PRESENTED TO:

_____

BY:

_____

DATE:

_____

To Dear Alana this Token
gift from me.

All my love

Josie

P.S Another please read
to her every morning
Thank you
love Josie

PURPOSE
for
EVERYDAY LIVING

Finding God in Your Everyday Life
365 Days a Year

CRISWELL FREEMAN

A Few Words of Introduction About God's Plans . . . And Yours

God has plans for you. Those plans are unfolding year by year, day by day, and moment by moment. If you keep your eyes *and* your heart open, every new day presents fresh opportunities to catch another glimpse of God's hand as it touches your life and guides your path.

Your Heavenly Father offers a continuous stream of blessings, all of which are intended to lead you to a place of spiritual abundance and peace. God is beckoning you to enjoy a closer relationship with Him, but He does not force Himself upon you. You are a creature of free will: You are free to embrace God's love, or not. You are free to obey His commandments, or not. You are free to welcome God's Son into your heart, or not. But remember this: Your attitude toward God will have a direct impact on every aspect of your life. The decisions that you make concerning your relationship to God have consequences that are profound *and* eternal, so decide carefully.

Sometimes, God's blessings are disguised as hardships; sometimes His gifts come in the form of unwelcome changes or bitter disappointments. Yet, even when the future seems unclear—or even when the future seems threatening—you can rest assured that your Heavenly Father is working *in* you and *through* you.

As you seek to gain a clearer understanding of God's plans for your life, here are a few points to consider:

1. Remember that the Search for Purpose Is a Journey, Not a Destination: Amid your changing circumstances, God will continue to reveal Himself to you if you sincerely seek His will. As you journey through the stages of life, remember that every new day presents fresh opportunities to seek God's will; make the conscious effort to seize those opportunities. Remember: God reveals Himself in the unspectacular moments of everyday life, so be watchful.

2. Pray Early and Often: Start each day with a time of prayer and devotional readings. In those quiet moments, God will lead you; your task, of course, is to be still, to seek His will, and to follow His direction.

3. Quiet Please: Sometimes, God speaks to you in a quiet voice; usually, the small quiet voice inside can help you find the right path for your life; listen to that voice.

4. Use All the Tools That God Provides: As you continue to make important decisions about your future, read God's Word every day, and consult with trusted advisors whom God has seen fit to place along your path.

5. Take Sensible Risks in Pursuit of Personal or Professional Growth: It is better to attempt noble undertakings and fail than to attempt nothing and succeed. But, do your best to avoid *foolish* risks. When in doubt, reread Proverbs.

6. Expect Setbacks: Your path will have many twists and turns. When you face a setback, don't become discouraged. When you encounter a roadblock, be prepared to make a U-turn. Then, start searching for a better route to your chosen destination.

7. Use Your Experiences as Valued Instructors: Philosopher George Santayana correctly observed, "Those who cannot remember the past are condemned to repeat it." Act accordingly.

8. Write It Down: If you're facing a big decision, or if you're searching for greater fulfillment from everyday life, begin keeping a daily journal. During quiet moments, make a written record of your thoughts, your goals, your hopes, and your concerns. The simple act of writing down your thoughts will help you clarify your ideas and your plans.

9. Don't Settle for Second, Third, of Fourth Best: God has big plans for you. Don't let Him down.

10. Serve Where You Stand: Even if you're not where you want to be, you *can* serve God exactly where you are. So don't underestimate the importance of your present work, and don't wait for a better day to serve God.

11. Find Pursuits About Which You Are Passionate: Find work that you love and causes that you believe in. You'll do your best when you become so wrapped up in something that you forget to call it work.

12. Have Faith and Get Busy: Remember the words of Cyrus Curtis: "Believe in the Lord and he will do half the work—the last half."

This book is a collection of scripture, devotional readings, and inspirational quotations that are intended to help you consider *God's* plan for *your* life. May these pages be a blessing to you and yours as you take the next important steps on your journey.

Criswell Freeman

YOUR PLANS, GOD'S PLANS

You will show me the path of life; in Your presence
is fullness of joy; at Your right hand
are pleasures forevermore.

Psalm 16:11 NKJV

✑ You have plans for your life, and so does God. And, as a Christian beginning a new year, you should ask yourself is this question: "How closely can I align my plans with God's plans?" The more closely you manage to follow the path that God intends for your life, the more you will benefit from the spiritual abundance that He offers to those who seek His will and obey His commandments.

Do you have questions or concerns about the coming year? Take them to God in prayer. Do you have hopes and dreams for the coming year? Entrust your hopes and dreams to Him. Are you carefully planning for the days and weeks ahead? Consult God as you establish your priorities. Turn every concern over to your Heavenly Father, and sincerely seek His guidance—prayerfully, earnestly, and often. Then, listen for His answers . . . and trust the answers that He gives.

✑ *One of the wonderful things about being a Christian is the knowledge that God has a plan for our lives.*

Warren Wiersbe

✑ *The greatest choice any man makes is to let God choose for him.*

Vance Havner

TRUSTING THE FUTURE TO GOD

*I say this because I know what I am planning
for you," says the Lord. "I have good plans for you,
not plans to hurt you. I will give you hope
and a good future."*

Jeremiah 29:11 NCV

◌ Because we are saved by a risen Christ, we can have hope for the future, no matter how troublesome our present circumstances may seem. After all, God has promised that we are His throughout eternity. And, He has told us that we must place our hopes in Him.

Are you willing to place your future in the hands of a loving and all-knowing God? Do you trust in the ultimate goodness of His plan for your life? Will you face today's challenges with optimism and hope? You should. After all, God created you for a very important purpose: His purpose. And you still have important work to do: His work.

Today, as you live in the present and look to the future, remember that God has a plan for you. Act—and believe—accordingly.

◌ *Never be afraid to trust an unknown future to a known God.*

Corrie ten Boom

◌ *The future is as bright as the promises of God.*

Adoniram Judson

NEW BEGINNINGS

*Then He who sat on the throne said,
"Behold, I make all things new."*

Revelation 21:5 NKJV

🔊 Today, like every other day, is literally brimming with possibilities. Whether we realize it or not, God is always working in us and through us; our job is to let Him do His work without undue interference. Yet, we are imperfect beings who, because of our limited vision, often resist God's will. We want life to unfold according to our own desires, not God's. But, our Heavenly Father may have other plans.

As you begin this new year, think carefully about the work that God can do through you. And then, set out upon the next phase of your life's journey with a renewed sense of purpose and hope. God has the power to make all things new, including you. Your job is to let Him do it.

🔊 *Consider every day as a new beginning, the first day of your life, and always act with the same fervor.*

Anthony of Padua

🔊 *Christ came when all things were growing old. He made them new.*

St. Augustine of Hippo

FIRST THINGS FIRST

Happy is the person who finds wisdom,
the one who gets understanding.

Proverbs 3:13 NCV

☙ "First things first." These words are easy to speak but hard to put into practice. For busy men and women living in a demanding world, placing first things first can be difficult indeed. Why? Because so many people are expecting so many things from us!

If you're having trouble prioritizing your day, perhaps you've been trying to organize your life according to your own plans, not God's. A better strategy, of course, is to take your daily obligations and place them in the hands of the One who created you. To do so, you must prioritize your day according to God's commandments, and you must seek His will and His wisdom in all matters. Then, you can face the day with the assurance that the same God who created our universe out of nothingness will help you place first things first in your own life.

☙ *Things which matter most must never be at the mercy of things which matter least.*

Goethe

☙ *You can't get second things by putting them first; you can get second things only by putting first things first.*

C. S. Lewis

ON GUARD AGAINST EVIL

Your love must be real. Hate what is evil,
and hold on to what is good.

Romans 12:9 NCV

❧ This world is God's creation, and it contains the wonderful fruits of His handiwork. But, it also contains countless opportunities to stray from God's will. Temptations are everywhere, and the devil, it seems, never takes a day off. Our task, as believers, is to turn away from temptation and to place our lives squarely in the center of God's will.

In his letter to Jewish Christians, Peter offered a stern warning: "The devil, your enemy, goes around like a roaring lion looking for someone to eat" (1 Peter 5:8 NCV). What was true in New Testament times is equally true in our own. Evil is indeed abroad in the world, and Satan continues to sow the seeds of destruction far and wide. As Christians, we must earnestly wrap ourselves in the protection of God's Holy Word. When we do, we are secure.

❧ *Do you know that often a root has split a rock when allowed to remain in it? Give no place to the seed of evil, seeing that it will break up your faith.*

Cyril of Jerusalem

❧ *The only thing necessary for the triumph of evil is for good men to do nothing.*

Edmund Burke

Sat

WHY AM I HERE?

May He grant you according to your heart's desire, and fulfill all your purpose.

Psalm 20:4 NKJV

⌖ "Why did God put me here?" It's an easy question to ask and, at times, a very difficult question to answer. As you seek to answer that question, God's purposes will not always be clear to you. Sometimes you may wander aimlessly in a wilderness of your own making. And sometimes, you may struggle mightily against God in a vain effort to find success and happiness through your own means, not His.

Are you earnestly seeking to discern God's purpose for your life? If so, these pages are intended as a reminder of several important facts: 1. God has a plan for your life; 2. If you seek that plan sincerely and prayerfully, you will find it; 3. When you discover God's purpose for your life, you will experience abundance, peace, joy, and power—God's power. And that's the only kind of power that really matters.

⌖ *Fear not that thy life shall come to an end, but rather that it shall never have a beginning.*

John Henry Cardinal Newman

⌖ *His life is our light—our purpose and meaning and reason for living.*

Anne Graham Lotz

TRUSTING GOD'S LOVE

For I am persuaded that neither death nor life, nor angels nor principalities nor powers, nor things present nor things to come, nor height nor depth, nor any other created thing, shall be able to separate us from the love of God which is in Christ Jesus our Lord.

Romans 8:38, 39 NKJV

√ God made you in His own image and gave you salvation through the person of His Son, Jesus Christ. And now, precisely because you are a wondrous creation treasured by God, a question presents itself: What will you do in response to the Creator's love? Will you ignore it or embrace it? Will you return it or neglect it? That decision, of course, is yours and yours alone.

When you embrace God's love, you are forever changed. When you embrace God's love, you feel differently about yourself, your neighbors, your family, and your world. More importantly, you share God's message—and His love—with others. Your Heavenly Father—a God of infinite love and mercy—is waiting to embrace you with open arms. Accept His love and trust His love . . . today and forever.

√ The greatest honor you can give Almighty God is to live gladly and joyfully because of the knowledge of His love.

Juliana of Norwich

ABUNDANCE IN THE YEAR AHEAD

*I have come that they may have life,
and that they may have it more abundantly.*

John 10:10 NKJV

❧ God offers us abundance, but He does not force it upon us. He promises that we "may have life" and that we "may have it more abundantly" if we accept His grace, His blessings, and His Son. When we entrust our hearts and our days to the One who created us, we experience abundance through the grace and sacrifice of His Son, Jesus. But, when we turn our thoughts and direct our energies away from God's commandments, we inevitably forfeit the spiritual abundance that might otherwise be ours.

Do you sincerely seek the riches that our Savior offers to those who give themselves to Him? Then follow Him completely and without reservation. When you do, you will receive the love and the abundance that He has promised.

❧ *God has promised us abundance, peace, and eternal life. These treasures are ours for the asking; all we must do is claim them. One of the great mysteries of life is why on earth do so many of us wait so very long to claim them?*

Marie T. Freeman

true

THE POWER OF HOPE

Be of good courage, and He shall strengthen
your heart, all you who hope in the Lord.

Psalm 31:24 NKJV

The self-fulfilling prophecy is alive, well, and living at your house. If you trust God and have faith for the future, your optimistic beliefs will give you direction and motivation. That's one reason that you should never lose hope, but certainly not the only reason. The primary reason that you, as a believer, should never lose hope, is because of God's unfailing promises.

Make no mistake about it, thoughts are powerful things: Your thoughts have the power to lift you up or to hold you down. When you acquire the habit of hopeful thinking, you will have acquired a powerful tool for improving your life. So, if you find yourself falling into the spiritual traps of worry and discouragement, seek the healing touch of Jesus and the encouraging words of fellow Christians. And, if you fall into the terrible habit of negative thinking, think again. After all, God's Word teaches us that Christ can overcome every difficulty (John 16:33). And when God makes a promise, He keeps it.

Hope is nothing more than the expectation of those things which faith has believed to be truly promised by God.

John Calvin

Wed

PRAYING FOR PURPOSE

Then He spoke a parable to them,
that men always ought to pray and not lose heart.

Luke 18:1 NKJV

❧ God's purpose for your life unfolds day by day. Each new morning offers fresh opportunities to study God's Word and seek His will. That's why it is vitally important that you take time for a daily chat with God. No habit is more important to your spiritual health than the discipline of daily prayer and devotion to your Creator.

Making a regular appointment with God—and keeping it—is an essential part of your daily journey with Christ. When you begin each day with your head bowed and your heart lifted, you are reminded of God's love, His protection, and His commandments. It is during these quiet moments with God you can align your priorities for the coming day with the teachings of His Holy Word.

Are you seeking a renewed sense of purpose for your life? Are you searching for answers to difficult questions? Would you like to embark upon a new spiritual pilgrimage? If so, ask for God's direction starting today . . . starting with your morning devotional.

❧ *When we pray, we have linked ourselves with Divine purposes, and we therefore have Divine power at our disposal for human living.*

E. Stanley Jones

ACCEPTING THE UNCHANGEABLE

Be of good courage, and let us be strong for
our people and for the cities of our God.
And may the Lord do what is good in His sight.

1 Chronicles 19:13 NKJV

❧ American Theologian Reinhold Niebuhr composed a profoundly simple verse that came to be known as the Serenity Prayer: "God, grant me the serenity to accept the things I cannot change, the courage to change the things I can, and the wisdom to know the difference." Niebuhr's words are far easier to recite than they are to live by. Why? Because most of us want life to unfold in accordance to our own wishes and timetables. But God may have a totally different plan, a plan that we cannot comprehend.

So if you've encountered unfortunate circumstances that are beyond your power to control, accept those circumstances . . . and trust God. When you do, you can be comforted in the knowledge that your Creator is both loving and wise, and that He understands His plans perfectly, even when you do not.

❧ *Tomorrow's job is fathered by today's acceptance. Acceptance of what, at least for the moment, you cannot alter.*

Max Lucado

In Search of Peace

Peace I leave with you, My peace I give to you;
not as the world gives do I give to you.
Let not your heart be troubled, neither let it be afraid.

John 14:27 NKJV

❧ The beautiful words of John 14:27 remind us that Jesus offers us peace, not as the world gives, but as He alone gives. When we accept the peace of Jesus Christ into our hearts, our lives are transformed. And then, because we possess the gift of peace, we can share that gift with fellow Christians, family members, friends, and associates. If, on the other hand, we choose to ignore the gift of peace—for whatever reason—we simply cannot share what we do not possess.

Today, as a gift to yourself, to your family, and to your friends, claim the inner peace that is your spiritual birthright: the peace of Jesus Christ. It is offered freely; it has been paid for in full; it is yours for the asking. So ask. And then share.

❧ *That peace, which has been described and which believers enjoy, is a participation of the peace which their glorious Lord and Master himself enjoys.*

Jonathan Edwards

❧ *The better you become acquainted with God, the less tensions you feel and the more peace you possess.*

Charles L. Alleni

MOUNTAIN-MOVING FAITH

_If you have faith as a mustard seed, you will say
to this mountain, 'Move from here to there,' and
it will move; and nothing will be impossible for you._

Matthew 17:20 NKJV

☙ Have you ever felt your faith in God slipping away? If so, you are not alone. Every life—including yours—is a series of successes and failures, celebrations and disappointments, joys and sorrows. But even when we feel very distant from God, God is never distant from us.

Jesus taught His disciples that if they had faith, they could move mountains. You can too. When you place your faith, your trust, indeed your life in the hands of Christ Jesus, you'll be amazed at the marvelous things He can do with you and through you. So strengthen your faith through praise, through worship, through Bible study, and through prayer. And trust God's plans. With Him, all things are possible, and He stands ready to open a world of possibilities to you if you have faith.

☙ _Faith in faith is pointless. Faith in a living, active God moves mountains._

Beth Moore

☙ _Only God can move mountains, but faith and prayer can move God._

E. M. Bounds

Sun

PRAISE FOR THE FATHER

*From the rising of the sun to its going down
the Lord's name is to be praised.*

Psalm 113:3 NKJV

❧ When is the best time to praise God? In church? Before dinner is served? When we tuck little children into bed? None of the above. The best time to praise God is all day, every day, to the greatest extent we can, with thanksgiving in our hearts.

Too many of us, even well-intentioned believers, tend to "compartmentalize" our waking hours into a few familiar categories: work, rest, play, family time, and worship. To do so is a mistake. Worship and praise should be woven into the fabric of everything we do; it should never be relegated to a weekly three-hour visit to church on Sunday morning.

Mrs. Charles E. Cowman, the author of the classic devotional text *Streams in the Desert*, wrote, "Two wings are necessary to lift our souls toward God: prayer and praise. Prayer asks. Praise accepts the answer." Today, find a little more time to lift your concerns to God in prayer, and praise Him for all that He has done. He's listening . . . and He wants to hear from you.

❧ *Be not afraid of saying too much in the praises of God; all the danger is of saying too little.*

Matthew Henry

Mon

A THANKFUL HEART

Enter into His gates with thanksgiving, and into His courts with praise. Be thankful to Him, and bless His name. For the Lord is good; His mercy is everlasting, and His truth endures to all generations.

Psalm 100:4, 5 NKJV

❧ Every good gift comes from God. As believers who have been saved by a risen Christ, we owe unending thanksgiving to our Heavenly Father. Yet sometimes, when everyday life begins to spin out of control, we simply don't stop to pause and thank our Creator for His countless gifts.

Are you taking God's gifts for granted? If so, you are doing a disservice to your Creator and to yourself. And the best way to resolve that problem is make this day a time for celebration and praise. Starting now.

❧ *No duty is more urgent than that of returning thanks.*

Ambrose of Milan

❧ *If you can't tell whether your glass is half-empty of half-full, you don't need another glass; what you need is better eyesight . . . and a more thankful heart.*

Marie T. Freeman

True

THE OPTIMISTIC CHRISTIAN

Make me hear joy and gladness.

Psalm 51:8 NKJV

As you take the next step in your life's journey, you should do so with feelings of hope and anticipation. After all, as a Christian, you have every reason to be optimistic about life. But, sometimes, rejoicing may be the last thing on your mind. Sometimes, you may fall prey to worry, frustration, anxiety, or sheer exhaustion. What's needed is plenty of rest, a large dose of perspective, and God's healing touch, but not necessarily in that order.

A. W. Tozer writes, "Attitude is all-important. Let the soul take a quiet attitude of faith and love toward God, and from there on, the responsibility is God's. He will make good on His commitments." These words remind us that even when the challenges of the day seem daunting, God remains steadfast. And, so must we.

No Christian can be a pessimist, for Christianity is a system of radical optimism.

William R. Inge

Christ can put a spring in your step and a thrill in your heart. Optimism and cheerfulness are products of knowing Christ.

Billy Graham

FINDING TIME FOR GOD

I am always praising you; all day long I honor you.

Psalm 71:8 NCV

☙ Each new day is a gift from God, and if we are wise, we spend a few quiet moments each morning thanking the Giver. Daily life is a tapestry of habits, and no habit is more important to our spiritual health than the discipline of daily prayer and devotion to the Creator. When we begin each day with heads bowed and hearts lifted, we remind ourselves of God's love, His protection, and His commandments. And if we are wise, we take time throughout the day to align our priorities with the teachings and commandments that God has given us through His Holy Word.

Are you thankful for God's blessings? Then give Him a gift that demonstrates your gratitude: the gift of time.

☙ *Half an hour of listening to God is essential except when one is very busy. Then, a full hour is needed.*

Francis of Sales

☙ *There is no way to draw closer to God unless you are in the Word of God every day. It's your compass. Your guide. You can't get where you need to go without it.*

Stormie Omartian

Thur

TRUSTING GOD'S PROVIDENCE

_Trust in the Lord with all your heart, and
lean not on your own understanding; in all your ways
acknowledge Him, and He shall direct your paths._

Proverbs 3:5, 6 NKJV

❧ When Jesus confronted the reality of His impending death on the cross, He asked God that this terrible burden might be lifted. But as He faced the possibility of profound suffering, Jesus prayed, "Nevertheless not my will, but Yours, be done" (Luke 22:42 NKJV). As Christians, we, too, must be willing to accept God's will, even when we do not fully understand the reasons for the hardships we must endure.

Grief and suffering visit all of us who live long and love deeply. When we lose a loved one, or when we experience any other profound loss, darkness overwhelms us for a while, and it seems as if we cannot summon the strength to face another day—but, with God's help, we can. When we confront circumstances that trouble us to the very core of our souls, we must trust God. When we are anxious, we must be still and listen for the quiet assurance of God's promises. And then, by placing our lives in His hands, we learn that God is our shepherd today and throughout eternity.

❧ _Trust the past to God's mercy, the present to God's love, and the future to God's providence._

St. Augustine of Hippo

KEEPING LIFE IN PERSPECTIVE

Incline your ear to wisdom,
and apply your heart to understanding.
Proverbs 2:2 NKJV

❧ Sometimes, amid the demands of daily life, we lose perspective. Life seems out of balance, and the pressures of everyday living seem overwhelming. What's needed is a fresh perspective, a restored sense of balance…and God.

If we call upon the Lord and seek to see the world through His eyes, He will give us guidance and wisdom and perspective. When we make God's priorities our priorities, He will lead us according to His plan and according to His commandments. God's reality is the ultimate reality. May we live accordingly.

❧ *When you and I hurt deeply, what we really need is not an explanation from God but a revelation of God. We need to see how great God is; we need to recover our lost perspective on life.*
Warren Wiersbe

❧ *Like a shadow declining swiftly away, like the dew of the morning gone with the heat of the day; so are our lives on earth when seen in light of eternity.*
Ruth Bell Graham

❧ *Live near to God, and all things will appear little to you in comparison with eternal realities.*
Robert Murray McCheyne

COURAGE FOR EVERYDAY LIVING

*For God has not given us a spirit of fear,
but of power and of love and of a sound mind.*
2 Timothy 1:7 NKJV

❧ Life here on earth can be difficult and discouraging at times. During our darkest moments, God offers us strength and courage if we turn our hearts and our prayers to Him.

As believing Christians, we have every reason to live courageously. After all, the ultimate battle has already been fought and won on the cross at Calvary. But sometimes, because we are imperfect human beings who possess imperfect faith, we fall prey to fear and doubt. The answer to our fears, of course, is God.

The next time you find your courage tested to the limit, remember that God is as near as your next breath. He is your shield and your strength; He is your protector and your deliverer. Call upon Him in your hour of need and then be comforted. Whatever your challenge, whatever your trouble, God can handle it . . . and will!

❧ *When once we are assured that God is good, then there can be nothing left to fear.*

Hannah Whitall Smith

❧ *Why rely on yourself and fall? Cast yourself upon His arm. Be not afraid. He will not let you slip.*

St. Augustine of Hippo

Sam

FINDING GOD'S PURPOSE IN EVERYDAY LIFE

*Have I not commanded you? Be strong and
of good courage; do not be afraid, nor be dismayed,
for the Lord your God is with you wherever you go.*

Joshua 1:9 NKJV

✑ Each morning, as the sun rises in the east, you welcome a new day, one that is filled to the brim with opportunities, with possibilities, and with God. As you contemplate God's blessings in your own life, you should prayerfully seek His guidance for the day ahead.

Discovering God's unfolding purpose for your life is a daily journey, a journey guided by the teachings of God's Holy Word. As you reflect upon God's promises and upon the meaning that those promises hold for you, ask God to lead you throughout the coming day. Let your Heavenly Father direct your steps; concentrate on what God wants you to do now, and leave the distant future in hands that are far more capable than your own: *His* hands.

✑ *If we are ever going to be or do anything for our Lord, now is the time.*

Vance Havner

✑ *Have I today done anything to fulfil the purpose for which Thou didst cause me to be born?*

John Baillie

THE BREAD OF LIFE

Then Jesus said, "I am the bread that gives life.
Whoever comes to me will never be hungry, and
whoever believes in me will never be thirsty."

John 6:35 NCV

❧ He was the Son of God, but He wore a crown of thorns. He was the savoir of mankind, yet He was put to death on roughhewn cross made of wood. He offered His healing touch to an unsaved world, and yet the same hands that had healed the sick and raised the dead were pierced with nails.

Jesus Christ, the Son of God, was born into humble circumstances. He walked this earth, not as a ruler of men, but as the Savior of mankind. His crucifixion, a torturous punishment that was intended to end His life and His reign, instead became the pivotal event in the history of all humanity.

Jesus is the bread of life. Accept His grace. Share His love. And follow His footsteps.

❧ *In all your deeds and words, you should look on Jesus as your model, whether you are keeping silence or speaking, whether you are alone or with others.*

Bonaventure

❧ *Jesus was the Savior Who would deliver them not only from the bondage of sin but also from meaningless wandering through life.*

Anne Graham Lotz

THE POWER OF EXPECTANT PRAYER

*Therefore I say to you, whatever things you ask
when you pray, believe that you receive them,
and you will have them.*

Mark 11:24 NKJV

✍ "The power of prayer": These words are so familiar, yet sometimes we forget what they mean. Prayer is powerful tool for communicating with our Creator; it is an opportunity to commune with Him. Prayer helps us find strength for today and hope for the future. Prayer is not a thing to be taken lightly or to be used infrequently.

Prayer should be an integral part of your daily life, not a hit-or-miss habit. The quality of your spiritual life will be in direct proportion to the quality of your prayer life. Prayer changes things, and it changes you. Today, instead of turning things over in your mind, turn them over to God in prayer. Instead of worrying about your next decision, ask God to lead the way. Don't limit your prayers to meals or to bedtime. Pray constantly about things great and small. God is listening, and He wants to hear from you now.

✍ *Whatever may be our circumstances in life, may each one of us really believe that by way of the Throne we have unlimited power.*

Annie Armstrong

WHEN IN DOUBT . . .

Don't depend on your own wisdom.
Respect the Lord and refuse to do wrong.

Proverbs 3:7 NCV

∽ Are you facing a difficult decision, a troubling circumstance, or a powerful temptation? If so, it's time to step back, to stop focusing on the world, and to focus, instead, on the will of your Father in heaven. The world will often lead you astray, but God will not. His counsel leads you to Himself, which, of course, is the path He has always intended for you to take.

Everyday living is an exercise in decision-making. Today and every day you must make choices: choices about what you will do, what you will worship, and how you will think. When in doubt, make choices that you sincerely believe will bring you to a closer relationship with God. And if you're uncertain of your next step, pray about it. When you do, answers will come. And you may rest assured that when God answers prayer, His answers are the right ones for you.

∽ God never turns away the honest seeker. Go to God with your questions. You may not find all the answers, but in finding God, you know the One who does.

Max Lucado

Putting Off Till Tomorrow

*If you make a promise to God, don't be slow
to keep it. God is not happy with fools,
so give God what you promised.*

Ecclesiastes 5:4 NCV

☙ The habit of procrastination takes a two-fold toll on its victims. First, important work goes unfinished; second, valuable energy is wasted in the process of putting off the things that remain undone. Procrastination results from an individual's shortsighted attempt to postpone temporary discomfort. What results is a senseless cycle of: 1. delay, followed by 2. worry, followed by 3. a panicky and often futile attempt to "catch up." Procrastination is, at its core, a struggle against oneself; the only antidote is action.

Once you acquire the habit of doing *what* needs to be done *when* it needs to be done, you will avoid untold trouble, worry, and stress. So, learn to defeat procrastination by paying less attention to your fears and more attention to your responsibilities. God has created a world that punishes procrastinators and rewards men and women who "do it now." In other words, life doesn't procrastinate. Neither should you.

☙ *Now is the only time worth having because, indeed, it is the only time we have.*

C. H. Spurgeon

DISCOVERING GOD'S PURPOSE IN TIMES OF ADVERSITY

These things I have spoken to you,
that in Me you may have peace. In the world
you will have tribulation; but be of good cheer,
I have overcome the world.

John 16:33 NKJV

❧ Whether we realize it or not, times of adversity can be times of intense personal and spiritual growth. Our difficult days are also times when we can learn and relearn some of life's most important lessons.

The next time you experience a difficult moment, a difficult day, or a difficult year, ask yourself this question: Where is God leading me? In times of struggle and sorrow, you can be certain that God is leading you to a place of His choosing. Your duty is to watch, to pray, to listen, and to follow.

❧ *When you feel that all is lost, sometimes the greatest gain is ready to be yours.*

Thomas à Kempis

❧ *It's a good thing to have all the props pulled out from under us occasionally. It gives us some sense of what rock is under our feet, and what is sand. It stops us from taking anything for granted.*

Madeleine L'Engle

Praising God's Glorious Creation

Then God saw everything that He had made,
and indeed it was very good.

Genesis 1:31 NKJV

❧ Today presents yet another opportunity to celebrate God's handiwork. Will you join in the celebration?

If you are wise, you won't just stop to "smell the roses." You will also pause and examine the exquisite details of God's glorious creation. When you do, you'll discover that the more carefully you inspect God's unfolding universe, the more beautiful it becomes.

❧ *Today, you will encounter God's creation. When you see the beauty around you, let each detail remind you to lift your head in praise.*

Max Lucado

❧ *Because God created the Natural—invented it out of His love and artistry—it demands our reverence.*

C. S. Lewis

❧ *God writes the gospel not in the Bible alone, but on the trees, and flowers, and clouds, and stars.*

Martin Luther

GOD'S TIMETABLE

To everything there is a season,
a time for every purpose under heaven.

Ecclesiastes 3:1 NKJV

✍ Most of us are impatient for God to grant us the desires of our heart. Usually, we know what we want, and we know precisely when we want it: right now, if not sooner. But when God's plans differ from our own, we must trust His infinite wisdom and His infinite love.

As busy men and women living in a fast-paced world, many of us find that waiting quietly for God is difficult. Why? Because we are fallible human beings seeking to live according to our own timetables, not God's. In our better moments, we realize that patience is not only a virtue, it is also the essence of wisdom and the foundation of trust.

✍ *Waiting is an essential part of spiritual discipline. It can be the ultimate test of faith.*

Anne Graham Lotz

✍ *Events of all sorts creep or fly exactly as God pleases.*

William Cowper

✍ *It's safe to trust God's methods and to go by His clock.*

S. D. Gordon

STRENGTH FOR TODAY

The Lord is my strength and song, and He has become my salvation; He is my God, and I will praise Him.

Exodus 15:2 NKJV

❧ Where do you turn for strength? Do you depend upon the world's promises or, for that matter, upon your own resources? Or do you turn toward God for the wisdom and strength to meet to challenges of the coming day? The answer should be obvious: God comes first.

Each morning, before you become caught up in the complexities of everyday life, spend meaningful moments with your Creator. Offer Him your prayers and study His Word. When you offer God the firstfruits of your day, you gain wisdom, perspective, and strength.

❧ *When God is our strength, it is strength indeed; when our strength is our own, it is only weakness.*

St. Augustine of Hippo

❧ *Sometimes I think spiritual and physical strength is like manna: you get just what you need for the day, no more.*

Suzanne Dale Ezell

❧ *Jesus is not a strong man making men and women who gather around Him weak. He is the Strong creating the strong.*

E. Stanley Jones

True

This Is the Day

This is the day the Lord has made;
we will rejoice and be glad in it.

Psalm 118:24 NKJV

❧ The words of Psalm 118 invite us to celebrate the gift of life. Yet sometimes we don't feel much like celebrating. Sometimes, life here on earth can be complicated, demanding, and frustrating. When the demands of life leave us rushing from place to place with scarcely a moment to spare, we may fail to pause and thank our Creator for the countless blessings He bestows upon us. But, whenever we neglect to give proper thanks to the Giver of all things good, we suffer because of our misplaced priorities.

As believers who have been saved by a risen Christ, we are blessed beyond human comprehension. We who have been given so much should make thanksgiving a habit, a regular part of our daily routines. Of course, God's gifts are too numerous to count, but we should attempt to count them, nonetheless. We owe our Heavenly Father everything, including our eternal praise . . . starting right now.

❧ *Why wait until the fourth Thursday in November? Why wait until the morning of December twenty-fifth? Thanksgiving to God should be an everyday affair. The time to be thankful is now!*

Jim Gallery

THE POWER OF OUR THOUGHTS

*Set your mind on things above,
not on things on the earth.*

Colossians 3:2 NKJV

❧ Our thoughts have the power to shape our lives—
for better or worse. Thoughts have the power to lift
our spirits, to improve our circumstances, and to
strengthen our relationship with the Creator. But,
our thoughts also have the power to cause us great
harm if we focus too intently upon those things
that distance us from God.

Today, make your thoughts an offering to God.
Seek—by the things you think and the actions you
take—to honor Him and serve Him. He deserves
no less. And neither, for that matter, do you.

❧ *The things we think are the things that feed our souls.
If we think on pure and lovely things, we shall grow pure
and lovely like them; and the converse is equally true.*

Hannah Whitall Smith

❧ *Just as clouds hide the sun, so bad thoughts cast
shadows over the soul.*

St. John Climacus

❧ *Good thoughts bear good fruit and bad thoughts bear
bad fruit. And a man is his own gardener.*

James Allen

GOD MAKES ALL THINGS POSSIBLE

You are the God who does wonders;
You have declared Your strength among the peoples.

Psalms 77:14 NKJV

❧ Sometimes, because we are imperfect human beings with limited understanding and limited faith, we place limitations on God. But, God's power has no limitations. God will work miracles in our lives *if* we trust Him with everything we have and everything we are. When we do, we experience the miraculous results of His endless love and His awesome power.

Do you lack the faith that God can work miracles in your own life? If so, it's time to reconsider. Are you a "Doubting Thomas," or a "Negative Nancy"? If so, you are attempting to place limitations on a God who has none. Instead, you must trust in God and trust in His power. Then, you must wait patiently . . . because something miraculous is just about to happen.

❧ *Too many Christians live below the miracle level.*

Vance Havner

❧ *I believe that God is in the miracle business—that his favorite way of working is to pick up where our human abilities and understandings leave off and then do something wondrous and unexpected.*

Emilie Barnes

IMITATING OUR SAVIOR

If you love Me, keep My commandments.

John 14:15 NKJV

❧ Imitating Christ is impossible, but *attempting to imitate Him* is both possible *and* advisable. By attempting to imitate Jesus, we seek, to the best of our abilities, to walk in His footsteps. To the extent we succeed in following Him, we receive the spiritual abundance that is the rightful possession of those who love Christ and keep His commandments.

Do you seek God's blessings for the day ahead? Then, to the best of your abilities, imitate His Son. You will fall short, of course. But if your heart is right and your intentions are pure, God will bless your efforts, your day, and your life.

❧ *A person who gazes and keeps on gazing at Jesus becomes like him in appearance.*

E. Stanley Jones

❧ *The whole idea of belonging to Christ is to look less and less like we used to and more and more like Him.*

Angela Thomas

❧ *Every Christian is to become a little Christ. The whole purpose of becoming a Christian is simply nothing else.*

C. S. Lewis

THE WISDOM OF SILENCE

My soul, wait silently for God alone,
For my expectation is from Him.

Psalms 62:5 NKJV

✐ Do you take time each day for an extended period of silence? And during those precious moments, do you sincerely open your heart to your Creator? If so, you are wise and you are blessed.

The world can be a noisy place, a place filled to the brim with distractions, interruptions, and frustrations. And if you're not careful, the struggles and stresses of everyday living can rob you of the peace that should rightfully be yours because of your personal relationship with Christ. So take time each day to quietly commune with your Savior. When you do, those moments of silence will enable you to participate more fully in the only source of peace that endures: God's peace.

✐ *I always begin my prayers in silence, for it is in the silence of the heart that God speaks.*

Mother Teresa

✐ *Because Jesus Christ is our Great High Priest, not only can we approach God without a human "go-between," we can also hear and learn from God in some sacred moments without one.*

Beth Moore

A PLAN FOR TODAY

Depend on the Lord in whatever you do,
and your plans will succeed.

Proverbs 16:3 NCV

✍ Would you like a formula for successful living that never fails? Here it is: Include God in every aspect of your life's journey, including the plans that you make and the steps that you take. But beware: As you make plans for the days and weeks ahead, you may become sidetracked by the demands of everyday living.

If you allow the world to establish your priorities, you will eventually become discouraged, or disappointed, or both. But if you genuinely seek God's will for every important decision that you make, your loving Heavenly Father will guide your steps and enrich your life. So, as you plan your work, remember that every good plan should start with God, including yours.

✍ *Plan your work. Without a system, you'll feel swamped.*

Norman Vincent Peale

✍ *God has a course mapped out for your life, and all the inadequacies in the world will not change His mind. He will be with you every step of the way. And though it may take time, He has a celebration planned for when you cross over the "Red Seas" of your life.*

Charles Swindoll

Mon

PUTTING POSSESSIONS IN PROPER PERSPECTIVE

No one can serve two masters. The person will hate
one master and love the other, or will follow
one master and refuse to follow the other.
You cannot serve both God and worldly riches.

Matthew 6:24 NCV

☙ On the grand stage of a well-lived life, material possessions should play a rather small role. Yet sometimes, we allow our possessions to assume undue control over our lives. God, of course, has other intentions, and so should we.

How much of your life are you investing in the pursuit of money and the things that money can buy? Do you own your possessions, or vice versa? Is your life ruled by the quest for earthly riches or the search for the spiritual kind?

If material possessions are ruling your life, rid yourself of them. After all, nothing on the face of this earth is important enough to separate you from your Creator. Absolutely nothing.

☙ *It's sobering to contemplate how much time, effort, sacrifice, compromise, and attention we give to acquiring and increasing our supply of something that is totally insignificant in eternity.*

Anne Graham Lotz

RECEIVING GOD
IN THE PRESENT TENSE

*You shall love the Lord your God with all your heart,
with all your soul, and with all your strength.*

Deuteronomy 6:5 NKJV

❧ God's love for you is deeper and more profound than you can imagine. God's love for you is so great that He sent His only Son to this earth to die for your sins and to offer you the priceless gift of eternal life. Now, you must decide whether or not to accept God's gift. Will you ignore it or embrace it? Will you return it or neglect it? Will you accept Christ's love and build a lifelong relationship with Him, or will you turn away from Him and take a different path?

Your decision to allow Christ to reign over your heart is the pivotal decision of your life. It is a decision that you cannot ignore. It is a decision that is yours and yours alone. Accept God's gift *now*: Allow His Son to preside over your heart, your thoughts, and your life, starting this very instant.

❧ *Jesus is the personal approach from the unseen God coming so near that he becomes inescapable. You don't have to find him—you just have to consent to be found.*

E. Stanley Jones

Wed

A SOCIETY BRIMMING
WITH TEMPTATIONS

*No temptation has overtaken you except such as is
common to man; but God is faithful, who will not
allow you to be tempted beyond what you are able,
but with the temptation will also make the way of
escape, that you may be able to bear it.*

1 Corinthians 10:13 NKJV

🔊 Here in the 21st century, the temptations of
our world are now completely and thoroughly
woven into the fabric of everyday life. So, if you're
looking for a way to be tempted or distracted, you
won't need to look very far. Thankfully, God has
promised that with His help, you can resist every
temptation that confronts you.

When you encounter the evils of this world—
and you will—use prayer as an antidote and
common sense as your guide. Turn your temptations
over to a Power much greater than your own. And
be comforted by the certain knowledge that no
challenge is too great for God, not even yours.

🔊 *Since you are tempted without ceasing, pray without
ceasing.*

C. H. Spurgeon

🔊 *Temptation always carries with it some bait that not
only attracts us, but also hides the fact that yielding to the
desire will eventually bring sorrow and punishment.*

Warren Wiersbe

THE JOYS OF FELLOWSHIP

*Then all the people went away to eat and drink,
to send some of their food to others, and to celebrate
with great joy. They finally understood
what they had been taught.*

Nehemiah 8:12 NCV

🕮 Fellowship with other believers should be an integral part of your everyday life. You association with fellow Christians should be uplifting, enlightening, encouraging, and consistent.

Are you an active member of your own fellowship? Are you a builder of bridges inside the four walls of your church *and* outside it? Do you contribute to God's glory by contributing your time and your talents to a close-knit band of believers? Hopefully so. The fellowship of believers is intended to be a powerful tool for spreading God's Good News and uplifting His children. And God intends that *you* be a fully contributing member that fellowship. Your intentions should be the same.

🕮 *Be united with other Christians. A wall with loose bricks is not good. The bricks must be cemented together.*

Corrie ten Boom

🕮 *One of the ways God refills us after failure is through the blessing of Christian fellowship. Just experiencing the joy of simple activities shared with other children of God can have a healing effect on us.*

Anne Graham Lotz

OBEDIENCE TO THE FATHER

*But be doers of the word, and not hearers only,
deceiving yourselves.*

James 1:22 NKJV

❧ God's commandments are not "suggestions," and they are not "helpful hints." They are, instead, immutable laws which, if followed, lead to repentance, salvation, and abundance. But if you choose to disobey the commandments of your Heavenly Father or the teachings of His Son, you will most surely reap a harvest of regret.

The formula for a successful life is surprisingly straightforward: Study God's Word and obey it. Does this sound too simple? Perhaps it is simple, but it is also the only way to reap the marvelous riches that God has in store for You.

❧ *Let your fellowship with the Father and with the Lord Jesus Christ have as its one aim and object a life of quiet, determined, unquestioning obedience.*

Andrew Murray

❧ *Let me tell you—there is no "high" like the elation and joy that come from a sacrificial act of obedience.*

Bill Hybels

❧ *Nobody is good by accident. No man ever became holy by chance.*

C. H. Spurgeon

OUR PROBLEMS =
GOD'S OPPORTUNITIES

*As for God, His way is perfect; the word of the Lord
is proven; He is a shield to all who trust in Him.*
Psalm 18:30 NKJV

✍ Here's a riddle: What is it that is *too
unimportant* to pray about yet *too big* for God to
handle? The answer, of course, is: "nothing." Yet
sometimes, when the challenges of the day seem
overwhelming, we may spend more time worrying
about our troubles than praying about them. We
may spend more time fretting about our problems
than solving them. A far better strategy is to pray
as if everything depended entirely upon God and to
work as if everything depended entirely upon us.

What we see as problems God sees as opportunities. And if we are to trust Him completely, we
must acknowledge that even when our own vision
is dreadfully impaired, His vision is perfect. Today
and every day, let us trust God by courageously
confronting the things that *we* see as problems and
He sees as possibilities.

✍ *Go forward confidently, energetically attacking
problems, expecting favorable outcomes.*
Norman Vincent Peale

✍ *We are all faced with a series of great opportunities,
brilliantly disguised as unsolvable problems. Unsolvable
without God's wisdom, that is.*
Charles Swindoll

GRACE FOR TODAY

My grace is sufficient for you,
for My strength is made perfect in weakness.

2 Corinthians 12:9 NKJV

❧ God's grace is not earned . . . thank goodness! To earn God's love and His gift of eternal life would be far beyond the abilities of even the most righteous man or woman. Thankfully, God's grace is not an earthly reward for righteous behavior; it is a blessed spiritual gift that can be accepted by believers who dedicate themselves to God through Christ. When we accept Christ into our hearts, we are saved by His grace.

As you contemplate the day ahead, praise God for His blessings. He is the Giver of all things good. He is the Comforter, the Protector, the Teacher, and the Savior. Praise Him today and forever.

❧ *The grace of God is sufficient for all our needs, for every problem, and for every difficulty, for every broken heart, and for every human sorrow.*

Peter Marshall

❧ *Marvelous, infinite, matchless grace, freely bestowed on all who believe! God's grace that will pardon and cleanse within!*

Julia H. Johnston

Scattering Seeds of Kindness

*Be kindly affectionate to one another with brotherly
love, in honor giving preference to one another;
not lagging in diligence, fervent in spirit,
serving the Lord; rejoicing in hope, patient in
tribulation, continuing steadfastly in prayer.*

Romans 12:10–12 NKJV

∾ What is a friend? The dictionary defines the
word friend as "a person who is attached to another
by feelings of affection or personal regard." This
definition is accurate, as far as it goes, but when we
examine the deeper meaning of friendship, so many
more descriptions come to mind: trustworthiness,
loyalty, helpfulness, kindness, understanding, forgiveness, encouragement, humor, and cheerfulness,
to mention but a few.

How wonderful are the joys of friendship. Today,
as you consider the many blessings that God has
given you, remember to thank Him for the friends
He has chosen to place along your path. May you
be a blessing to them, and may they richly bless you
today, tomorrow, and every day that you live.

∾ *That's a good part of the good old days—to be
genuinely interested in your neighbor, and if you hear a
distress signal, go see about him and his problem.*

Jerry Clower

FOLLOWING IN THE FOOTSTEPS

Whoever serves me must follow me.
Then my servant will be with me everywhere I am.
My Father will honor anyone who serves me.

John 12:26 NCV

☙ Jesus walks with you. Are you walking with Him? If you are wise, you will choose to walk with Him today and every day of your life. Jesus loved you so much that He endured unspeakable humiliation and suffering for you. How will you respond to Christ's sacrifice? Will you take up His cross and follow Him?

When you place your hopes squarely at the foot of the cross, when you place Jesus squarely at the center of your life, you will be blessed. The old familiar hymn begins, "What a friend we have in Jesus...." No truer words were ever written. Jesus is the sovereign friend and ultimate savior of mankind. Christ showed enduring love for His believers by willingly sacrificing His own life so that we might have eternal life. Now, it is our turn to become His friend.

☙ *The heaviest end of the cross lies ever on His shoulders. If He bids us carry a burden, He carries it also.*

C. H. Spurgeon

☙ *A believer comes to Christ; a disciple follows after Him.*

Vance Havner

CELEBRATING LIFE

Rejoice in the Lord, O you righteous!
For praise from the upright is beautiful.

Psalm 33:1 NKJV

❧ Do you approach each day with celebration or with reservation? If you are a believer who has been redeemed by a loving Savior, the answer should be obvious. Each day should be a cause for celebration and for praise.

Thoughtful Christians should be joyful Christians. And even on life's darker days, even during those difficult times when we scarcely see a single ray of sunlight, we can still praise God and thank Him for our blessings. When we do, we demonstrate that our acquaintance with the Master is not a passing fancy but is, instead, the cornerstone and the touchstone of our lives.

❧ *Christ and joy go together.*

E. Stanley Jones

❧ *Some of us seem so anxious about avoiding hell that we forget to celebrate our journey toward heaven.*

Philip Yancey

❧ *A child of God should be a visible beatitude for joy and a living doxology for gratitude.*

C. H. Spurgeon

thru

TRUSTING GOD'S WORD

Man shall not live by bread alone, but by every word that proceeds from the mouth of God.

Matthew 4:4 NKJV

❧ The Bible is unlike any other book. A. W. Tozer wrote, "The purpose of the Bible is to bring men to Christ, to make them holy and prepare them for heaven. In this it is unique among books, and it always fulfills its purpose."

As Christians, we are called upon to share God's Holy Word with a world in desperate need of His healing hand. The Bible is a priceless gift, a tool for Christians to use as they share the Good News of their Savior, Christ Jesus. Too many Christians, however, keep their spiritual tool kits tightly closed and out of sight.

Jonathan Edwards advised, "Be assiduous in reading the Holy Scriptures. This is the fountain whence all knowledge in divinity must be derived. Therefore let not this treasure lie by you neglected." God's Holy Word is, indeed, a priceless, one-of-a-kind treasure. Handle it with care, but more importantly, handle it every day.

❧ *Weave the unveiling fabric of God's word through your heart and mind. It will hold strong, even if the rest of life unravels.*

Gigi Graham Tchividjian

WHAT KIND OF EXAMPLE?

Be an example to the believers in word, in conduct,
in love, in spirit, in faith, in purity.

1 Timothy 4:12 NKJV

❧ As followers of Christ, we must each ask ourselves an important question: "What kind of example am I?" The answer to that question determines, in large part, whether or not we are positive influences on our own little corners of the world.

Are you the kind of friend whose life serves as a powerful example of righteousness? Are you a person whose behavior serves as a positive role model for young people? Are you the kind of Christian whose actions, day in and day out, are based upon integrity, fidelity, and a love for the Lord? If so, you are not only blessed by God, you are also a powerful force for good in a world that desperately needs positive influences such as yours.

Phillips Brooks advised, "Be such a person, and live such a life, that if every person were such as you, and every life a life like yours, this earth would be God's Paradise." And that's sound advice because our families and friends are watching . . . and so, for that matter, is God.

❧ *Preach the gospel at all times and, if necessary, use words.*

Francis of Assisi

EARTHLY PRESSURES
AND THE SPIRITUAL PATH

We say they are happy because they did not give up.
You have heard about Job's patience, and you know
the Lord's purpose for him in the end.
You know the Lord is full of mercy and is kind.

James 5:11 NCV

❧ Our world is filled with pressures: some good, some bad. The pressures that we feel to follow God's will and obey His commandments are positive pressures. God places them on our hearts, and He intends that we act in accordance with His leadings. But we also face different pressures, ones that are definitely *not* from God. When we feel pressured to do things—or even to think thoughts—that lead us *away* from God, we must beware.

Society seeks to mold us into more worldly beings; God seeks to mold us into new beings, new creations through Christ, beings that are most certainly *not* conformed to this world. If we are to please God, we must resist the pressures that society seeks to impose upon us, and we must conform ourselves, instead, to His will, to His path, and to His Son.

❧ *Only the man who follows the command of Jesus single-mindedly and unresistingly lets his yoke rest upon him, finds his burden easy, and under its gentle pressure receives the power to persevere in the right way.*

Dietrich Bonhoeffer

MORE OPPORTUNITIES THAN WE CAN COUNT

Jesus said to him, "If you can believe,
all things are possible to him who believes."

Mark 9:23 NKJV

❧ Whether you realize it or not, opportunities are whirling around you like stars crossing the night sky: beautiful to observe but too numerous to count. Yet you may be too wrapped up in the daily grind to notice.

Take time to step back from the challenges of everyday living so that you can focus you thoughts on two things: the talents God has given you *and* the opportunities that He has placed before you. God is leading you in the direction of those opportunities. Your task is to watch carefully, to pray fervently, and to act accordingly.

❧ *The world is round, and the place which may seem like the end may also be only the beginning.*

Ivy Baker Priest

❧ *Unbelief keeps us living beneath the possibilities that God dreamed for our lives.*

Angela Thomas

❧ *You don't just luck into things; you build step by step, whether it's friendships or opportunities.*

Barbara Bush

Mon

ABOVE AND BEYOND OUR WORRIES

> *So don't worry about tomorrow,*
> *because tomorrow will have its own worries.*
> *Each day has enough trouble of its own.*
>
> *Matthew 6:34* NCV

✍ Because we are fallible human beings, we worry. Even though we, as Christians, have the assurance of salvation—even though we, as Christians, have the promise of God's love and protection—we find ourselves fretting over the countless details of everyday life. Jesus understood our concerns when he spoke the reassuring words found in the 6th chapter of Matthew.

Perhaps you are concerned about the inevitable challenges of everyday life. Perhaps you are uncertain about your future or your finances. Or perhaps you are simply a "worrier" by nature. If so, make Matthew 6 a regular part of your daily Bible reading. This beautiful passage will remind you that God still sits in His heaven and you are His beloved child. Then, perhaps, you will worry a little less and trust God a little more, and that's as it should be because God is trustworthy…and you are protected.

✍ *Worry is interest paid on trouble before it comes due.*

William Ralph Inge

✍ *Worry does not empty tomorrow of its sorrow; it empties today of its strength.*

Corrie ten Boom

PRAYER: MORE IS BETTER

Rejoice always, pray without ceasing,
in everything give thanks; for this is the will
of God in Christ Jesus for you.

1 Thessalonians 5:16–18 NKJV

✒ Genuine, heartfelt prayer changes things *and* it changes us. When we lift our hearts to our Father in heaven, we open ourselves to a never-ending source of divine wisdom and infinite love.

Do you have questions that you simply can't answer? Ask for the guidance of your Father in heaven. Whatever your need, no matter how great or small, pray about it. Instead of waiting for mealtimes or bedtimes, follow the instruction of your Savior: Pray always and never lose heart. And remember: God is not just near; He is here, and He's ready to talk with you. Now.

✒ *Aspire to God with short but frequent outpourings of the heart; admire His bounty; invoke His aid; cast yourself in spirit at the foot of His cross; adore His goodness; treat with Him of your salvation; give Him your whole soul a thousand times in the day.*

Francis of Sales

✒ *The Christian prays in every situation, in his walks for recreation, in his dealing with others, in silence, in reading, in all rational pursuits.*

Clement of Alexandria

Wed

WHEN THE PATH IS DARK

When I sit in darkness, the Lord will be a light to me.

Micah 7:8 NKJV

☞ Throughout the seasons of life, we must all endure life-altering personal losses that leave us breathless. When we do, we may be overwhelmed by fear, by doubt, or by both. Thankfully, God has promised that He will never desert us. And God keeps His promises.

Life is often challenging, but as Christians, we must trust the promises of our Heavenly Father. God loves us, and He will protect us. In times of hardship, He will comfort us; in times of sorrow, He will dry our tears. When we are troubled, or weak, or sorrowful, God is with us. His love endures, not only for today, but also for all of eternity.

☞ *Dark as my path may seem to others, I carry a magic light in my heart. Faith, the spiritual strong searchlight, illumines the way, and although sinister doubts lurk in the shadow, I walk unafraid toward the enchanted wood where the foliage is always green, where joy abides, where nightingales nest and sing, and where life and death are one in the presence of the Lord.*

Helen Keller

☞ *Where there is no longer any opportunity for doubt, there is no longer any opportunity for faith, either.*

Paul Tournier

TRUSTING YOUR CONSCIENCE

And do not be conformed to this world,
but be transformed by the renewing of your mind,
that you may prove what is that good and acceptable
and perfect will of God.

Romans 12:2 NKJV

ℐ❧ Billy Graham correctly observed, "Most of us follow our conscience as we follow a wheelbarrow. We push it in front of us in the direction we want to go." To do so, of course, is a profound mistake. Yet all of us, on occasion, have failed to listen to the voice that God planted in our hearts, and all of us have suffered the consequences.

God gave you a conscience for a very good reason: to make your path conform to His will. Wise believers make it a practice to listen carefully to that quiet internal voice. Count yourself among that number. When your conscience speaks, listen and learn. In all likelihood, God is trying to get His message through. And in all likelihood, it is a message that you desperately need to hear.

ℐ❧ *Many words do not satisfy the soul; but a good life eases the mind and a clean conscience inspires great trust in God.*

Thomas à Kempis

ℐ❧ *God's law enters our mind and draws it to itself by stirring up conscience, which itself is called the law of our mind.*

St. John of Damascus

LIVING AND WORKING PASSIONATELY

In all the work you are doing, work the best you can.
Work as if you were doing it for the Lord,
not for people.

Colossians 3:23 NCV

🖉 Are you passionate about your life, your loved ones, your work, and your faith? As a believer who has been saved by a risen Christ, you should be.

As a thoughtful Christian, you have every reason to be enthusiastic about life, but sometimes the struggles of everyday living may cause you to feel decidedly unenthusiastic. If you feel that your zest for life is slowly fading away, it's time to slow down, to rest, to count your blessings, and to pray. When you feel worried or weary, you must pray fervently for God to renew your sense of wonderment and excitement.

Life with God is a glorious adventure; revel in it. When you do, God will most certainly smile upon your work and your life.

🖉 *When the dream of our heart is one that God has planted there, a strange happiness flows into us. At that moment, all of the spiritual resources of the universe are released to help us. Our praying is then at one with the will of God and becomes a channel for the Creator's purposes for us and our world.*

Catherine Marshall

HOW THEY KNOW
THAT WE KNOW HIM

*Now by this we know that we know Him,
if we keep His commandments.*

1 John 2:3 NKJV

✍ How do others know that we are followers of Christ? By our words and by our actions. And when it comes to proclaiming our faith, the actions we take are far more important than the proclamations we make.

Is your conduct a worthy example for believers and non-believers alike? Is your behavior a testimony to the spiritual abundance that is available to those who allow Christ to reign over their hearts? If so, you are wise: congratulations. But if you're like most of us, then you know that some important aspect of your life could stand improvement. If so, today is the perfect day to make yourself a living, breathing example of the wonderful changes that Christ can make in the lives of those who choose to walk with Him.

✍ *Let us remember therefore this lesson: That to worship our God sincerely we must evermore begin by hearkening to His voice, and by giving ear to what He commands us. For if every man goes after his own way, we shall wander. We may well run, but we shall never be a whit nearer to the right way, but rather farther away from it.*

John Calvin

Sun

THE COMPANY YOU KEEP

Do not be deceived:
"Evil company corrupts good habits."

1 Corinthians 15:33 NKJV

❧ Some friendships help us honor God; these friendships should be nurtured. Other friendships place us in situations where we are tempted to dishonor God by disobeying His commandments; friendships that dishonor God have the potential to do us great harm.

Because we tend to become like our friends, we must choose our friends carefully. Because our friends influence us in ways that are both subtle and powerful, we must ensure that our friendships are pleasing to God. When we spend our days in the presence of godly believers, we are blessed, not only by those friends, but also by our Creator.

Do you seek to live a life that is pleasing to God? If so, you should build friendships that are pleasing to Him. When you do, your Heavenly Father will bless you and your friends with gifts that are simply too numerous to count.

❧ *Tell me what company you keep, and I'll tell you what you are.*

Miguel de Cervantes

❧ *If you choose to awaken a passion for God, you will have to choose your friends wisely.*

Lisa Bevere

MARY, MARTHA, AND THE MASTER

You will teach me how to live a holy life.
Being with you will fill me with joy;
at your right hand I will find pleasure forever.

Psalm 16:11 NCV

Martha and Mary were sisters who both loved Jesus, but they showed their love in different ways. Mary sat at the Master's feet, taking in every word. Martha, meanwhile, busied herself with preparations for the meal to come. When Martha asked Jesus if He was concerned about Mary's failure to help, Jesus replied, "Mary has chosen the better thing, and it will never be taken away from her." (Luke 10:42 NCV). The implication is clear: As believers, we must spend time *with* Jesus before we spend time *for* him. But, once we have placed Christ where He belongs—at the center of our hearts—we must go about the business of serving the One who has saved us.

How can we serve Christ? By sharing His message, His mercy, and His love with those who cross our paths. Everywhere we look, it seems, the needs are great and so are the temptations. Still, our challenge is clear: We must love God, obey His commandments, trust His Son, and serve His children. When we do, we claim spiritual treasures that will endure forever.

The crucial question for each of us is this: What do you think of Jesus, and do you yet have a personal acquaintance with Him?

Hannah Whitall Smith

DAY BY DAY WITH GOD

Uphold my steps in Your paths,
that my footsteps may not slip.

Psalms 17:5 NKJV

❧ Our world is in a state of constant change. God is not. At times, the world seems to be trembling beneath our feet. But we can be comforted in the knowledge that our Heavenly Father is the rock that cannot be shaken. His Word promises, "I am the Lord, I do not change" (Malachi 3:6 NKJV).

Every day we live, we encounter a multitude of changes—some good, some not so good. At all times, our loving Father stands ready to protect us, to comfort us, to guide us, and, in time, to heal us.

Are you facing difficult circumstances or unwelcome changes? If so, please remember that God is far bigger than any problem you may face. So, instead of worrying about life's inevitable challenges, put your faith in the Father and His only begotten Son: Jesus Christ is the same yesterday, today, and forever (Hebrews 13:8). And rest assured: It is precisely because your Savior does not change that you can face your challenges with courage for this day and hope for the future.

❧ *Don't be overwhelmed. Take it one day and one prayer at a time.*

Stormie Omartian

REALLY LIVING MEANS
REALLY LOVING

*And may the Lord make you increase
and abound in love to one another and to all.*
1 Thessalonians 3:12 NKJV

Christ's words are clear: We are to love God first, and secondly, we are to love others as we love ourselves (Matthew 22:37–40). These two commands are seldom easy, and because we are imperfect beings, we often fall short. But God's Holy Word commands us to try.

The Christian path is an exercise in love and forgiveness. If we are to walk in Christ's footsteps, we must forgive those who have done us harm, and we must accept Christ's love by sharing it freely with family, friends, neighbors, and strangers.

You will find, as you look back upon your life, that the moments when you have really lived are the moments when you have done things in the spirit of love.
Henry Drummond

Each year some new heart finally hears, finally sees, finally knows love, and in heaven, there is great rejoicing! The Child is born anew, and one more knee is bowed!
Ann Weems

When the evening of this life comes, we shall be judged on love.
John of the Cross

Thur

PRAYERFUL PATIENCE

The Lord is good to those who wait for Him,
To the soul who seeks Him. It is good that
one should hope and wait quietly
For the salvation of the Lord.

Lamentations 3:25, 26 NKJV

  Lamentations 3:25, 26 reminds us that it is good to wait quietly for God. But for most of us, waiting patiently for Him is difficult. Why? Because we are fallible human beings with a long list of earthly desires and a definite timetable for obtaining them.

The next time you find yourself impatiently waiting for God to reveal Himself, remember that the world unfolds according to His timetable, not ours. Sometimes, we must wait, and when we do, we should do so quietly and patiently. And, as we consider God's love for us and the perfection of His plans, we can be comforted in the certain knowledge that *His* timing is perfect, even if *our* patience is not.

  To receive the blessing we need, we must believe and keep on believing, to wait and keep on waiting. We need to wait in prayer, wait with our Bibles open as we confess his promises, wait in joyful praise and worship of the God who will never forget our case, and wait as we continue serving others in his name.

Jim Cymbala

A HUMBLE SPIRIT

The greatest among you must be a servant.
But those who exalt themselves will be humbled,
and those who humble themselves will be exalted.

Matthew 23:11, 12 NKJV

✍ Sometimes our faith is tested more by prosperity than by adversity. Why? Because in times of plenty, we are tempted to stick out our chests and say, "I did that." But nothing could be further from the truth. All of our blessings start and end with God; whatever "it" is, He did it. And He deserves the credit.

Who are the greatest among us? Are they the proud and the powerful? Hardly. The greatest among us are the humble servants who care less for their own glory and more for God's glory. If we seek greatness in God's eyes, we must forever praise His good works, not our own.

✍ *Nothing sets a person so much out of the devil's reach as humility.*

Jonathan Edwards

✍ *We see how Jesus clearly chooses the way of humility. He does not appear with great fanfare as a powerful savior, announcing a new order. On the contrary, he comes quietly, with the many sinners who are receiving a baptism of repentance.*

Henri Nouwen

ASKING AND ACCEPTING

So I say to you, ask, and it will be given to you; seek, and you will find; knock, and it will be opened to you. For everyone who asks receives, and he who seeks finds, and to him who knocks it will be opened.

Luke 11:9, 10 NKJV

✐ God gives the gifts; we, as believers, should accept them—but oftentimes, we don't. Why? Because we fail to trust our Heavenly Father completely, and because we are, at times, surprisingly stubborn. Luke 11 teaches us that God does not withhold spiritual gifts from those who ask. Our obligation, quite simply, is to ask for them.

Are you asking God to move mountains in your life, or are you expecting Him to stumble over molehills? Whatever the size of your challenges, God is big enough to handle them. Ask for His help today, with faith and with fervor, and then watch in amazement as your mountains begin to move.

✐ *All we have to do is to acknowledge our need, move from self-sufficiency to dependence, and ask God to become our hiding place.*

Bill Hybels

✐ *You need not cry very loudly: he is nearer to us than we think.*

Brother Lawrence

QUESTIONS AND ANSWERS

Listen carefully to wisdom;
set your mind on understanding.

Proverbs 2:2 NCV

✍ Life presents each of us with countless questions, conundrums, doubts, and problems. Thankfully, the riddles of everyday living are not too difficult to solve *if* we look for answers in the right places. When we have questions, we should consult God's Word, we should seek the guidance of the Holy Spirit, and we should trust the counsel of God-fearing friends and family members.

Are you facing a difficult decision? Take your concerns to God and avail yourself of the messages and mentors that He has placed along your path. When you do, God will speak to you in His own way and in His own time, and when He does, you can most certainly trust the answers that He gives.

✍ *It is the nature and the advantage of strong people that they can bring out the crucial questions and form a clear opinion about them. The weak always have to decide between alternatives that are not their own.*

Dietrich Bonhoeffer

✍ *If you are struggling to make some difficult decisions right now that aren't specifically addressed in the Bible, don't make a choice based on what's right for someone else. You are the Lord's and He will make sure you do what's right.*

Lisa Whelchel

Mon

BUILDING CHARACTER, MOMENT BY MOMENT

Let integrity and uprightness preserve me,
for I wait for You.

Psalm 25:21 NKJV

❧ Character is built slowly over a lifetime. It is the sum of every right decision, every honest word, every noble thought, and every heartfelt prayer. It is forged on the anvil of honorable work and polished by the twin virtues of generosity and humility. Character is a precious thing—difficult to build but easy to tear down. As believers in Christ, we must seek to live each day with discipline, honesty, and faith. When we do, integrity becomes a habit. And God smiles.

❧ *Character is made in the small moments of our lives.*

Phillips Brooks

❧ *Character is formed by doing the thing we are supposed to do, when it should be done, whether we feel like doing it or not.*

Father Flanagan

❧ *Integrity is the glue that holds our way of life together. When wealth is lost, nothing is lost; when health is lost, something is lost; when character is lost, all is lost.*

Billy Graham

LOVE GOD AND GET BUSY

And let us not grow weary while doing good, for in due season we shall reap if we do not lose heart.

Galatians 6:9 NKJV

The old saying is both familiar and true: Actions speak louder than words. And as believers, we must beware: Our actions should always give credence to the changes that Christ can make in the lives of those who walk with Him.

God calls upon each of us to act in accordance with His will and with respect for His commandments. If we are to be responsible believers, we must realize that it is never enough simply to hear the instructions of God; we must also live by them. And it is never enough to wait idly by while others to do God's work here on earth; we, too, must act. Doing God's work is a responsibility that each of us must bear, and when we do, our loving Heavenly Father rewards our efforts with a bountiful harvest.

Remember that the Christian life is one of action, not of speech and daydreams. Let there be few words and many deeds, and let them be done willingly.

Vincent Pallotti

Action springs not from thought, but from a readiness for responsibility.

Dietrich Bonhoeffer

Ned

FINDING THE PURPOSE
BENEATH THE PROBLEM

Be joyful because you have hope.
Be patient when trouble comes,
and pray at all times.

Romans 12:12 NCV

Hidden beneath every problem is the seed of a solution—God's solution. Your challenge, as a faithful believer, is to trust God's providence and seek His solutions. When you do, you will eventually discover that God does nothing without a very good reason: *His* reason.

Are you willing to faithfully trust God on good days *and* bad ones? Hopefully so, because an important part of walking with God is finding *His* purpose in the midst of *your* problems.

Underneath each trouble there is a faithful purpose.

C. H. Spurgeon

Looking back, I can see that the most exciting events of my life have all risen out of trouble.

Catherine Marshall

Let God's promises shine on your problems.

Corrie ten Boom

Living in an Anxious World

*Be anxious for nothing, but in everything by prayer
and supplication, with thanksgiving,
let your requests be made known to God.*

Philippians 4:6 NKJV

We live in a world that often breeds anxiety
and fear. When we come face-to-face with tough
times, we may fall prey to discouragement, doubt,
or depression. But our Father in Heaven has other
plans. God has promised that we may lead lives of
abundance, not anxiety. In fact, His Word instructs
us to "be anxious for nothing." But how can we put
our fears to rest? By taking those fears to God and
leaving them there.

As you face the challenges of everyday living,
do you find yourself becoming anxious, troubled,
discouraged, or fearful? If so, turn every one of your
concerns over to your Heavenly Father. The same
God who created the universe will comfort you *if*
you ask Him…so ask Him and trust Him. And then
watch in amazement as your anxieties melt into the
warmth of His loving hands.

*The beginning of anxiety is the end of faith, and the
beginning of true faith is the end of anxiety.*

George Mueller

*Anxiety does not empty tomorrow of its sorrows,
but it empties today of its strength.*

C. H. Spurgeon

HOLINESS BEFORE HAPPINESS

Blessed are those who hunger and thirst for
righteousness, for they shall be filled.

Matthew 5:6 NKJV

☙ Because you are an imperfect human being, you are not "perfectly" happy—and that's perfectly okay with God. He is far less concerned with your happiness than He is with your holiness.

God continuously reveals Himself in everyday life, but He does not do so in order to make you contented; He does so in order to lead you to His Son. So don't be overly concerned with your current level of happiness: It will change. Be more concerned with the current state of your relationship with Christ: He does not change. And because your Savior transcends time and space, you can be comforted in the knowledge that in the end, His joy will become your joy . . . for all eternity.

☙ *God saved us to make us holy, not happy.*

Vance Havner

☙ *Holiness isn't in a style of dress. It's not a matter of rules and regulations. It's a way of life that emanates quietness and rest, joy in family, shared pleasures with friends, the help of a neighbor – and the hope of a Savior.*

Joni Eareckson Tada

HE IS HERE

*Every morning he wakes me. He teaches me to listen
like a student. The Lord God helps me learn…*

Isaiah 50:4, 5 NCV

❧ We live in a fast-paced world. The demands
of everyday life can seem overwhelming at times,
but when we slow ourselves down and seek the
presence of a loving God, we do a wonderful thing:
we invite His peace into our hearts.

Do you set aside quiet moments each day to
offer praise to your Creator? You should. During
these moments of stillness, you will often sense the
infinite love and power of our Lord.

The familiar words of Psalm 46:10 remind us to
"Be still, and know that I am God." (NKJV). When
we do so, we encounter the awesome presence of
our loving Heavenly Father, and we are comforted
in the knowledge that God is not just near. He is
here.

*❧ God makes prayer as easy as possible for us. He's
completely approachable and available, and He'll never
mock or upbraid us for bringing our needs before Him.*

Shirley Dobson

*❧ There is nothing more important in any life than
the constantly enjoyed presence of the Lord. There
is nothing more vital, for without it we shall make
mistakes, and without it we shall be defeated.*

Alan Redpath

Sun

LIVING ON PURPOSE

*God chose you to be his people, so I urge you now to
live the life to which God called you.*

Ephesians 4:1 NCV

✒ Life is best lived on purpose. And purpose, like
everything else in the universe, begins with God.
Whether you realize it or not, God has a plan for
your life, a divine calling, a direction in which He
is leading you. When you welcome God into your
heart and establish a genuine relationship with
Him, He will begin, in time, to make His purposes
known.

Sometimes, God's intentions will be clear to
you; other times, God's plan will seem uncertain
at best. But even on those difficult days when you
are unsure which way to turn, you must never lose
sight of these overriding facts: God created you for
a reason; He has important work for you to do; and
He's waiting patiently for you to do it.

The next step is up to you.

✒ *Without God, life has no purpose, and without
purpose, life has no meaning.*

Rick Warren

✒ *The really committed leave the safety of the harbor
and set their compasses for the place of total devotion to
God, and whatever life adventures He plans for them.*

Bill Hybels

HELPING THE HELPLESS

I have shown you in every way, by laboring like this,
that you must support the weak. And remember
the words of the Lord Jesus, that He said,
"It is more blessed to give than to receive."

Acts 20:35 NKJV

☙ The words of Jesus are unambiguous: "Freely you have received, freely give" (Matthew 10:8 NKJV). As followers of Christ, we are commanded to be generous with our friends, with our families, and *especially* with those in need. We must give freely of our time, our possessions, and our love.

In 2 Corinthians 9, Paul reminds us "God loves a cheerful giver." (v. 7 NKJV). So take God's words to heart and make this pledge: Be a cheerful, generous, and courageous giver. The world needs your help, and you need the spiritual rewards that will be yours when you do.

☙ *If we can enter the church day and night and implore God to hear our prayers, how careful we should be to hear and grant the petitions of our neighbors in need.*

Francis of Assisi

☙ *To show great love for God and our neighbor, we need not do great things. It is how much love we put in the doing that makes our offering something beautiful for God.*

Mother Teresa

THE PEACEFUL,
PRODUCTIVE CHRISTIAN LIFE

Do all you can to live a peaceful life. Take care of your own business, and do your own work as we have already told you. If you do, then people who are not believers will respect you, and you will not have to depend on others for what you need.

1 Thessalonians 4:11, 12 NCV

Attending to your job and caring for your family requires work and plenty of it. But God is not complaining, and neither should you.

God's Holy Word is clear: He rewards diligence. As believers, we are instructed to be disciplined, steadfast, and industrious.

Our Heavenly Father has created a world in which hard work is honored and idleness is not. We reside in that world, so we must live—and work—accordingly.

The world does not consider labor a blessing, therefore it flees and hates it, but the pious who fear the Lord labor with a ready and cheerful heart, for they know God's command, and they acknowledge His calling.

Martin Luther

You will always have joy in the evening if you spend the day fruitfully.

Thomas à Kempis

FACING OUR FEARS

Fear not, for I have redeemed you;
I have called you by your name; You are Mine.

Isaiah 43:1 NKJV

✍ All of us may find our courage tested by the inevitable disappointments and tragedies of life. After all, ours is a world filled with uncertainty, hardship, sickness, and danger. Old Man Trouble, it seems, is never too far from the front door, so when we focus upon our fears and our doubts, we may find many reasons to lie awake at night and fret about the uncertainties of the coming day. A better strategy, of course, is to focus not upon our fears, but instead upon our God.

God is as near as your next breath, and He is in control. He offers salvation to all His children, including you. God is your shield and your strength; you are His forever. So don't focus your thoughts upon the fears of the day. Instead, trust God's plan and His eternal love for you. And remember: God is good, and He always has the last word.

✍ Are you fearful? First, bow your head and pray for God's strength. Then, raise your head knowing that, together, you and God can handle whatever comes your way.

Jim Gallery

THE LIFE OF MODERATION

Who is wise and understanding among you?
Let him show by good conduct that his works
are done in the meekness of wisdom.

James 3:13 NKJV

When we allow our appetites to run wild, they usually do. When we abandon moderation and focus, instead, on accumulation, we forfeit the inner peace that God offers—but does not guarantee—to His children. When we live intemperate lives, we rob ourselves of countless blessings that would have otherwise been ours.

God's instructions are clear: If we seek to live wisely, we must be moderate in our appetites and disciplined in our behavior. To do otherwise is an affront to Him . . . and to ourselves.

The soul that journeys to God, but doesn't shake off its cares and quiet its appetites, is like someone who drags a cart uphill.

John of the Cross

Virtue—even attempted virtue—brings light; indulgence brings fog.

C. S. Lewis

If thou would be happy, have an indifference for more than what is sufficient.

William Penn

WHEN CHANGE IS PAINFUL

We are hard pressed on every side, yet not crushed;
we are perplexed, but not in despair.

2 Corinthians 4:8 NKJV

🌿 When life unfolds according to our wishes, or when we experience unexpected good fortune, we find it *easy* to praise God's plan. That's when we greet change with open arms. But sometimes the changes that we must endure are painful. When we struggle through the difficult days of life, as we must from time to time, we may ask ourselves, "Why me?" The answer, of course, is that God knows, but He isn't telling . . . yet.

Have you endured a difficult transition that has left your head spinning or your heart broken? If so, you have a clear choice to make: Either you can cry and complain, or you can trust God and get busy fixing what's broken. The former is a formula for disaster; the latter is a formula for a well-lived life.

🌿 *Pain is the fuel of passion—it energizes us with an intensity to change that we don't normally possess.*

Rick Warren

🌿 *More often than not, when something looks like it's the absolute end, it is really the beginning.*

Charles Swindoll

Prosperity, Promises, and Peace

The Lord's blessing brings wealth,
and no sorrow comes with it.

Proverbs 10:22 NCV

✒ We live in an era of prosperity, a time when many of us have been richly blessed with an assortment of material possessions that our forebears could have scarcely imagined. As believers living in these prosperous times, we must be cautious: We must keep prosperity in perspective.

The world stresses the importance of material possessions; God does not. The world offers the promise of happiness through wealth and public acclaim; God offers the promise of peace through His Son.

When in doubt, we must distrust the world and trust God. The world often makes promises that it cannot keep, but when God makes a promise, He keeps it, not just for a day or a year or a lifetime, but for all eternity.

✒ *There is nothing wrong with people possessing riches. The wrong comes when riches possess people.*

Billy Graham

✒ *Wealth is something entrusted to us by God, something God doesn't want us to trust. He wants us to trust Him.*

Warren Wiersbe

NAVIGATING DEAD END STREETS

He gives power to the weak, and to those
who have no might He increases strength.

Isaiah 40:29 NKJV

🕮 As we travel the roads of life, all of us are confronted with streets that seem to be dead ends. When we do, we may become discouraged. After all, we live in a society where expectations can be high and demands even higher.

If you find yourself enduring difficult circumstances, remember that God remains in His heaven. If you become discouraged with the direction of your day or your life, turn your thoughts and prayers to Him. He is a God of possibility, not negativity. He will guide you through your difficulties and beyond them. And then, with a renewed spirit of optimism and hope, you can thank the Giver of all things good for gifts that are simply too profound to fully understand and for treasures that are too numerous to count.

🕮 *The stops of a good man are ordered by the Lord as well as his steps.*

George Mueller

🕮 *God never hurries. There are no deadlines against which He must work. To know this is to quiet our spirits and relax our nerves.*

A. W. Tozer

TIME FOR REST

*Come to Me, all you who labor and are heavy laden,
and I will give you rest. Take My yoke upon you
and learn from Me, for I am gentle and lowly in heart,
and you will find rest for your souls.
For My yoke is easy and My burden is light.*

Matthew 11:28–30 NKJV

❧ Even the most inspired Christians can, from time to time, find themselves "running out of steam." If you currently fit that description, remember that God expects you to do your work, but He also intends for you to rest. When you fail to take time for sufficient rest, you do a disservice to yourself, to your family, and to your coworkers.

Is your energy on the wane? Is your spiritual tank near empty? Are your emotions frayed? If so, it's time to turn your thoughts and your prayers to God. And when you're finished, it's time to treat yourself to a heaping helping of "R&R", which stands for "Rest and Renewal."

❧ *Prescription for a happier and healthier life: resolve to slow down your pace; learn to say no gracefully; resist the temptation to chase after more pleasure, more hobbies, and more social entanglements.*

James Dobson

❧ *Work is not always required. There is such a thing as sacred idleness.*

George MacDonald

A LIFE OF PRAYER

_Let the words of my mouth and the meditation
of my heart be acceptable in Your sight, O Lord,
my strength and my Redeemer._

Psalm 19:14 NKJV

✍ Is prayer an integral part of your daily life or is it a hit-or-miss habit? Do you "pray without ceasing," or is your prayer life an afterthought? Do you regularly pray in the solitude of the early morning darkness, or do you bow your head only when others are watching?

The quality of your spiritual life will be in direct proportion to the quality of your prayer life. Pray constantly about things great and small. God is always listening; it's up to you to do the rest.

✍ _A life growing in its purity and devotion will be a more prayerful life._

E. M. Bounds

✍ _The Christian on his knees sees more than the philosopher on tiptoe._

D. L. Moody

✍ _If you can't seem to forgive someone, pray for that person and keep praying for him or her until, with God's help, you've removed the poison of bitterness from your heart._

Marie T. Freeman

PUTTING FAITH TO THE TEST

Even though good people may be bothered by trouble seven times, they are never defeated.

Proverbs 24:16 NCV

Life is a tapestry of good days and difficult days, with good days predominating. During the good days, we are tempted to take our blessings for granted (a temptation that we must resist with all our might). But, during life's difficult days, we discover precisely what we're made of. And more importantly, we discover what *our faith* is made of.

Has your faith been put to the test yet? If so, then you know that with God's help, you can endure life's darker days. But if you have not yet faced the inevitable trials and tragedies of life-here-on-earth, don't worry: you will. And when you faith is put to the test, rest assured that God is perfectly willing—and always ready—to give you strength for the struggle.

The kind of faith that will not stand all types of weather is worth nothing.

C. H. Spurgeon

A faith that hasn't been tested can't be trusted.

Adrian Rogers

SHARING THE GOOD NEWS

Go therefore and make disciples of all the nations,
baptizing them in the name of the Father and of
the Son and of the Holy Spirit, teaching them to
observe all things that I have commanded you; and lo,
I am with you always, even to the end of the age.

Matthew 28:19, 20 NKJV

After His resurrection, Jesus addressed his disciples. As recorded in the 28th chapter of Matthew, Christ instructed His followers to share His message with the world. This "Great Commission" applies to Christians of every generation, including our own.

As believers, we are called to share the Good News of Jesus with our families, with our neighbors, and with the world. Christ commanded His disciples to become fishers of men. We must do likewise, and we must do so today. Tomorrow may indeed be too late.

Angels cannot preach the gospel; only beings such as Paul and you and I can preach the gospel.

Oswald Chambers

The evangelistic harvest is always urgent. The destiny of men and of nations is always being decided.

Billy Graham

God had an only Son and He made Him a missionary.

David Livingstone

THE PATH

*But grow in the grace and knowledge of our Lord
and Savior Jesus Christ.
To Him be the glory both now and forever.*

2 Peter 3:18 NKJV

🖋 Today, you will take one more step on your life's journey. Today offers one more opportunity to seek God's will and to follow it. Today has the potential to be a time of praise, a time of thanksgiving, and a time of spiritual abundance. The coming day is a canvass upon which you can compose a beautiful work of art *if* you choose to do so.

If you choose to follow in the footsteps of the One from Galilee, you will continue to mature every day of your life. If you choose to walk along the path that was first walked by Jesus, your life will become a masterpiece, a powerful work of art, and a tribute to your Savior. So today, as a gift to yourself, to your loved ones, and to your God, walk the path that Jesus walked.

🖋 *Grow, dear friends, but grow, I beseech you, in God's way, which is the only true way.*

Hannah Whitall Smith

🖋 *When it comes to walking with God, there is no such thing as instant maturity. God doesn't mass produce His saints. He hand tools each one, and it always takes longer than we expected.*

Charles Swindoll

The Way We Treat
Our Neighbors

The whole law is made complete in this one command:
"Love your neighbor as you love yourself."

Galatians 5:14 NCV

❧ How should we treat other people? God's Word is clear: We should treat others in the same way that we wish to be treated. This Golden Rule is easy to understand, but sometimes it can be difficult to live by.

Because we are imperfect human beings, we are, on occasion, selfish, thoughtless, or cruel. But God commands us to behave otherwise. He teaches us to rise above our own imperfections and to treat others with unselfishness and love. When we observe God's Golden Rule, we help build His kingdom here on earth. And, when we share the love of Christ, we share a priceless gift; may we share it today, tomorrow, and every day after that.

❧ *There are only two duties required of us—the love of God and the love of our neighbor, and the surest sign of discovering whether we observe these duties is the love of our neighbor.*

St. Teresa of Avila

❧ *If my heart is right with God, every human being is my neighbor.*

Oswald Chambers

HAPPINESS IS . . .

Happy are the people who live at your Temple . . . .
Happy are those whose strength comes from you.

Psalms 84:4, 5 NKJV

✒ Do you seek happiness, abundance, and contentment? If so, here are some things you should do: Love God and His Son; depend upon God for strength; try, to the best of your abilities, to follow God's will; and strive to obey His Holy Word. When you do these things, you'll discover that happiness goes hand-in-hand with righteousness. The happiest people are not those who rebel against God; the happiest people are those who love God and obey His commandments.

What does life have in store for you? A world full of possibilities (of course it's up to you to seize them), and God's promise of abundance (of course it's up to you to accept it). So, as you embark upon the next phase of your journey, remember to celebrate the life that God has given you. Your Creator has blessed you beyond measure. Honor Him with your prayers, your words, your deeds, *and* your joy.

✒ *Happiness is obedience, and obedience is happiness.*

C. H. Spurgeon

✒ *In happiness is brought to others, our own happiness is reflected.*

Father Flanagan

CHOICES PLEASING TO GOD

*I am offering you life or death, blessings or curses.
Now, choose life! Then you and your children
may live. To choose life is to love the Lord your God,
obey him, and stay close to him.*

Deuteronomy 30:19, 20 NCV

❧ Because we are creatures of free will, we make choices—lots of them. When we make choices that are pleasing to our Heavenly Father, we are blessed. When we make choices that cause us to walk in the footsteps of God's Son, we enjoy the abundance that Christ has promised to those who follow Him. But when make choices that are displeasing to God, we sow seeds that have the potential to bring forth a bitter harvest.

Today, as you encounter the challenges of everyday living, you will make hundreds of choices. Choose wisely. Make your thoughts and your actions pleasing to God. And remember: Every choice that is displeasing to Him is the wrong choice—no exceptions.

❧ *Whatever weakens your reason, impairs the tenderness of your conscience, obscures your sense of God, or removes your relish for spiritual things—that is sin to you.*

Susanna Wesley

MIRACLES GREAT AND SMALL

For with God nothing will be impossible.

Luke 1:37 NKJV

God is a miracle worker. Throughout history He has intervened in the course of human events in ways that cannot be explained by science or human rationale. And he's still doing so today.

God's miracles are not limited to special occasions, nor are they witnessed by a select few. God is crafting His wonders all around us: the miracle of the birth of a new baby; the miracle of a world renewing itself with every sunrise; the miracle of lives transformed by God's love and grace. Each day, God's handiwork is evident for all to see and experience.

Today, seize the opportunity to inspect God's hand at work. His miracles come in a variety of shapes and sizes, so keep your eyes and your heart open. Be watchful, and you'll soon be amazed.

Are you looking for a miracle? If you keep your eyes wide open and trust in God, you won't have to look very far.

Marie T. Freeman

There is Someone who makes possible what seems completely impossible.

Catherine Marshall

A CHANGE OF HEART

He who covers his sins will not prosper, but
whoever confesses and forsakes them will have mercy.
Proverbs 28:13 NKJV

℘ Who among us has sinned? All of us. But, God calls upon us to turn away from sin by following His commandments. And the good news is this: When we do ask God's forgiveness and turn our hearts to Him, He forgives us absolutely and completely.

Genuine repentance requires more than simply offering God apologies for our misdeeds. Real repentance may start with feelings of sorrow and remorse, but it ends only when we turn away from the sin that has heretofore distanced us from our Creator. In truth, we offer our most meaningful apologies to God, not with our words, but with our actions. As long as we are still engaged in sin, we may be "repenting," but we have not fully "repented."

Is there an aspect of your life that is distancing you from your God? If so, ask for His forgiveness, and—just as importantly—stop sinning. Then, wrap yourself in the protection of God's Word. When you do, you will be secure.

℘ *Repentance involves a radical change of heart and mind in which we agree with God's evaluation of our sin and then take specific action to align ourselves with His will.*

Henry Blackaby

SMALL ACTS OF KINDNESS

*Assuredly, I say to you, inasmuch as you did it to one
of the least of these My brethren, you did it to Me.*

Matthew 25:40 NKJV

In the busyness and confusion of daily life, it is easy to lose focus, and it is easy to become frustrated. We are imperfect human beings struggling to manage our lives as best we can, but we often fall short. When we are distracted or disappointed, we may neglect to share a kind word or a kind deed. This oversight hurts others, but it hurts us most of all.

Today, slow yourself down and be alert for those who need your smile, your kind words, or your helping hand. Make kindness a centerpiece of your dealings with others. They will be blessed, and you will be too.

Be faithful in the little practices of love which will build in you the life of holiness and will make you Christlike.

Mother Teresa

You will accomplish more by kind words and a courteous manner than by anger and sharp rebuke, which should never be used, except in necessity.

Angela Merici

In a battle of wills, loving kindness is the only weapon that conquers.

Vimalia McClure

MISTAKES:
THE PRICE OF BEING HUMAN

*Then they cried out to the Lord in their trouble,
and He saved them out of their distresses.*

Psalm 107:13 NKJV

We are imperfect beings living in an imperfect world; mistakes are simply part of the price we pay for being here. Yet, even though mistakes are an inevitable part of life's journey, *repeated* mistakes should not be. When we commit the inevitable blunders of life, we must correct them, learn from them, and pray for the wisdom to avoid those same mistakes in the future. If we are successful, our missteps become lessons, and our lives become adventures in growth.

Mistakes are the price we pay for being human; *repeated* mistakes are the price we pay for being stubborn. But, if we are wise enough to learn from our experiences, we continue to mature throughout every stage of life. And that's precisely what God intends for us to do.

It is human to err; it is devilish to remain willfully in error.

Augustine of Hippo

I hope you don't mind me telling you all this? One can learn only by seeing one's mistakes.

C. S. Lewis

THE PLAN ACCORDING TO GOD

*I will instruct you and teach you in the way
you should go; I will guide you with My eye.*

Psalms 32:8 NKJV

✒ Perhaps you have a clearly defined plan for the future, but even if you don't, rest assured that God does. God's has a definite plan for every aspect of your life. Your challenge is straightforward: To sincerely pray for God's guidance, and to obediently follow the guidance you receive.

If you're burdened by the demands of everyday life here in the 21st century, you are not alone. Life is difficult at times, and uncertain. But of this you can be sure: God has a plan for you and yours. He will communicate His plans using the Holy Spirit, His Holy Word, and your own conscience. So listen to God's voice and be watchful for His signs: He will send you messages every day of your life, including this one. Your job is to listen, to learn, to trust, and to act.

✒ *God has a plan for the life of every Christian. Every circumstance, every turn of destiny, all things work together for your good and for His glory.*

Billy Graham

✒ *It's incredible to realize that what we do each day has meaning in the big picture of God's plan.*

Bill Hybels

ETERNAL LIFE:
GOD'S PRICELESS GIFT

These things I have written to you who believe
in the name of the Son of God, that you may know
that you have eternal life.

1 John 5:13 NKJV

✍ Christ sacrificed His life on the cross so that we might have eternal life. This gift, freely given from God's only begotten Son, is the priceless possession of everyone who accepts Him as Lord and Savior.

God is waiting patiently for each of us to accept the gift of eternal life. Let us claim Christ's gift today. Let us walk with the Savior, let us love Him, let us praise Him, and let us share His message of salvation with the world.

✍ *This short, earthly life, important and significant though it may be in its setting, is no more than a prelude to a share in the timeless Life of God.*

J. B. Phillips

✍ *Someday you will read in the papers that Moody is dead. Don't you believe a word of it. At that moment I shall be more alive than I am now. I was born of the flesh in 1837, I was born of the spirit in 1855. That which is born of the flesh may die. That which is born of the Spirit shall live forever.*

D. L. Moody

OUR FAMILIES ARE WATCHING

*You must choose for yourselves today whom
you will serve . . . as for me and my family,
we will serve the Lord.*

Joshua 24:15 NCV

✒ Whether you realize it or not, you are serving as a powerful example to the members of your family. This raises an important question: What sort of example are you? Are you the kind of believer whose words and deeds are consistent? And do those words and deeds honor the One who gave His life on a cross so that you might enjoy life eternal?

As you encounter the challenges of everyday living, you will have many opportunities to serve as a powerful example of righteousness; seize those opportunities, starting today. Because your family is carefully watching—and constantly learning.

✒ *A person ought to live so that everybody knows he is a Christian, and most of all, his family ought to know.*

D. L. Moody

✒ *We can talk about faith, but what we live shows the true faith behind the words.*

Jay Kesler

✒ *You can preach a better sermon with your life than with your lips.*

Oliver Goldsmith

POSSESSED BY FAITH

*The Good News shows how God makes people
right with himself—that it begins and ends with faith.
As the Scripture says, "But those who are right
with God will live by trusting in him."*

Romans 1:17 NCV

Can you honestly say that you are an enthusiastic believer? Are you passionate about your faith and excited about your path? Hopefully so. But if your zest for life has waned, it is now time to redirect your efforts and recharge your spiritual batteries. And that means refocusing your priorities by putting God first.

Nothing is more important than your wholehearted commitment to your Creator and to His only begotten Son. Your faith must never be an afterthought; it must be your ultimate priority, your ultimate possession, and you ultimate passion.

I do not want merely to possess a faith; I want a faith that possesses me.

Charles Kingsley

When we wholeheartedly commit ourselves to God, there is nothing mediocre or run-of-the-mill about us. To live for Christ is to be passionate about our Lord and about our lives.

Jim Gallery

TIME: THE FABRIC OF LIFE

*Lord, tell me when the end will come
and how long I will live. Let me know how long
I have. You have given me only a short life . . . .
Everyone's life is only a breath.*

Psalms 39:4, 5 NCV

☙ Every day, like every life, is composed of moments. Each moment of your life holds within it the potential to seek God's will and to serve His purposes. If you are wise, you will strive to do both.

An important part of wisdom is the wise use of time. How will you invest your time today? Will you savor the moments of your life, or will you squander them? Will you use your time as an instrument of God's will, or will you allow commonplace distractions to rule your day and your life?

The gift of time is a gift from God. Treat it as if it were a precious, fleeting, one-of-a-kind treasure. Because it is.

☙ *Time wasted is a theft from God.*

Henri Frédéric Amiel

☙ *The choices of time are binding in eternity.*

Jack MacArthur

MAKING THE MOST OF OUR TALENTS

Do not neglect the gift that is in you.

1 Timothy 4:14 NKJV

All of us possess special gifts—bestowed from the Father above—and you are no exception. But, your gift is no guarantee of success; it must be cultivated and nurtured; otherwise, it will go unused . . . and God's gift to you will be squandered.

Today, make a promise to yourself that you will earnestly seek to discover the talents that God has given you. Then, nourish those talents and make them grow. Finally, vow to share your gifts with the world for as long as God gives you the power to do so. After all, the best way to say "Thank You" for God's gifts is to use them.

Employ whatever God has entrusted you with, in doing good, all possible good, in every possible kind and degree.

John Wesley

One thing taught large in the Holy Scriptures is that while God gives His gifts freely, He will require a strict accounting of them at the end of the road. Each man is personally responsible for his store, be it large or small, and will be required to explain his use of it before the judgment seat of Christ.

A. W. Tozer

WORDS WORTHY OF OUR SAVIOR

*When you talk, do not say harmful things,
but say what people need—words that will help
others become stronger. Then what you say will
do good to those who listen to you.*

Ephesians 4:29 NCV

❧ It is, indeed, the Golden Rule for Christians of every generation: "Therefore, whatever you want men to do to you, do also to them, for this is the Law and the Prophets" (Matthew 7:12 NKJV). If we are to observe the Golden Rule, we must be careful to speak words of encouragement, hope, and truth to all who cross our paths.

Sometimes, when we feel uplifted and secure, it easy to speak kind words. Other times, when we are discouraged or tired, we can scarcely summon the energy to uplift ourselves, much less anyone else. But, God's commandment is clear: We must observe the Golden Rule "in everything."

God intends that we speak words of kindness, wisdom, and truth, no matter our circumstances, no matter our emotions. When we do, we share a priceless gift with the world, and we give glory to the One who gave His life for us. As believers, we must do no less.

❧ When you talk, choose the very same words that you would use if Jesus were looking over your shoulder. Because He is.

Marie T. Freeman

A NEW DAY, A NEW PATH

Now that you are obedient children of God do not live as you did in the past. You did not understand, so you did the evil things you wanted. But be holy in all you do, just as God, the One who called you, is holy.

1 Peter 1:14, 15 NCV

✍ How will you respond to Christ's sacrifice? Will you take up His cross and follow Him (Luke 9:23) or will you choose another path? When you place Jesus squarely at the center of your life, and place your hopes in Him, you will be blessed.

The 19th-century writer Hannah Whitall Smith observed, "The crucial question for each of us is this: What do you think of Jesus, and do you yet have a personal acquaintance with Him?" Indeed, the answer to that question determines the quality, the course, and the direction of our lives today and for all eternity.

Let us put down our old ways and pick us His cross. Let us walk the path that He walked.

✍ Lord, I am no longer my own, but Yours. Let me be employed by You or laid aside for You, exalted for You or brought low by You. Let me have all things, let me have nothing. I freely and heartily yield all things to Your pleasure and disposal. And now, O glorious and blessed God, Father, Son, and Holy Spirit, You are mine and I am Yours. So be it. Amen.

John Wesley

Sun

CHRISTIANITY HERE AND NOW

Teach me to do Your will, for You are my God;
Your Spirit is good.
Lead me in the land of uprightness.

Psalms 143:10 NKJV

For believers, every day presents fresh opportunities to worship God though our prayers, through our praise, and though our service. And as Christians, we must remember that the appropriate moment to pray, to praise, and to serve is the present one.

If we are to honor God, we must begin by honoring Him now, not later. God is with us in the present moment, and we must strive to be with Him. "Now" is God's gift to us; hopefully, we will make it our gift to Him.

If a man cannot be a Christian in the place where he is, he cannot be a Christian anywhere.

Henry Ward Beecher

The whole essence of the spiritual life consists in recognizing the designs of God for us at the present moment.

Elisabeth Elliot

The one word in the spiritual vocabulary is now.

Oswald Chambers

EXPECTING GOD'S BLESSINGS

My cup runs over. Surely goodness and mercy shall
follow me all the days of my life;
and I will dwell in the house of the Lord forever.

Psalm 23:5, 6 NKJV

☙ To be a pessimistic Christian is a contradiction in terms, yet sometimes even the most devout Christians fall prey to fear, doubt, and discouragement. But, God has a different plan for our lives. The comforting words of the 23rd Psalm remind us of God's blessings. In response to His grace, we should strive to focus our thoughts on things that are pleasing to Him, not upon things that are evil, discouraging, or frustrating.

So, the next time you find yourself mired in the pit of pessimism, remember God's Word and redirect your thoughts. This world is God's creation; look for the best in it, and trust Him to take care of the rest.

☙ *It is when we give ourselves to be a blessing that we can specially count on the blessing of God.*

Andrew Murray

☙ *God is the giver, and we are the receivers. And His richest gifts are bestowed not upon those who do the greatest things, but upon those who accept His abundance and His grace.*

Hannah Whitall Smith

ANSWERED PRAYERS

He heeded their prayer,
because they put their trust in him.

1 Chronicles 5:20 NKJV

🕉 God answers our prayers. What God *does not* do is this: He does not answer our prayers in a time and fashion of *our* choosing, and He does not always answer our prayers *in the affirmative*. Sometimes our loving Heavenly Father responds to our requests by saying "No," and we must accept His answer, even though we may not understand it.

God answers prayers not according to *our* wishes but according to *His* master plan. We cannot know that plan, but we can know the Planner . . . and we must trust His wisdom, His righteousness, and His unending love.

🕉 *What God gives in answer to our prayers will always be the thing we most urgently need, and it will always be sufficient.*

Elisabeth Elliot

🕉 *The Lord's answers to prayer are infinitely perfect, and they will show that often when we were asking for a stone that looked like bread, He was giving us bread that to our shortsightedness looked like stone.*

J. Southley

BEYOND BITTERNESS

Those who show mercy to others are happy,
because God will show mercy to them.

Matthew 5:7 NCV

◿ Are you mired in the quicksand of bitterness or regret? If so, you are not only disobeying God's Word, you are also wasting your time. The world holds few if any rewards for those who remain angrily focused upon the past. Still, the act of forgiveness is difficult for all but the most saintly men and women.

Being frail, fallible, imperfect human beings, most of us are quick to anger, quick to blame, slow to forgive, and even slower to forget. Yet as Christians, we are commanded to forgive others, just as we, too, have been forgiven.

If there exists even one person—alive or dead—against whom you hold bitter feelings, it's time to forgive. Or, if you are embittered against yourself for some past mistake or shortcoming, it's finally time to forgive yourself and move on. Hatred, bitterness, and regret are not part of God's plan for your life. Forgiveness is.

◿ Give me such love for God and men as will blot out all hatred and bitterness.

Dietrich Bonhoeffer

LESSONS IN LEADERSHIP

Shepherd God's flock, for whom you are responsible.
Watch over them because you want to,
not because you are forced. That is how God wants it.
Do it because you are happy to serve.

1 Peter 5:2 NCV

✒ John Maxwell writes, "Great leaders understand that the right attitude will set the right atmosphere, which enables the right response from others." If you are in a position of leadership—whether as a parent or as a leader at your work, your church, or your school—it's up to you to set the right tone by maintaining the right attitude.

What's your attitude today? Are you fearful, angry, bored, or worried? Are you confused, bitter or pessimistic? If so, then you should ask yourself if you're the kind of leader whom you would want to follow.

Our world needs Christian leadership, and so do your family members and coworkers. You can become a trusted, competent, thoughtful leader *if* you learn to maintain the right attitude: one that realistic, optimistic, forward looking, and Christ-centered.

✒ *When God wants to accomplish something, He calls dedicated men and women to challenge His people and lead the way.*

Warren Wiersbe

TRUSTING THE QUIET VOICE

In quietness and confidence shall be your strength.

Isaiah 30:15 NKJV

🕯 Whenever you're about to make an important decision, you should listen carefully to the quiet voice inside. Sometimes, of course, it's tempting to do otherwise. From time to time you'll be tempted to abandon your better judgement by ignoring your conscience. Don't do it. Instead of ignoring that quiet little voice, pay careful attention to it. If you do, your conscience will lead you in the right direction—in fact, it's trying to lead you right now. So listen . . . and learn.

🕯 *It is neither safe nor prudent to do anything against conscience.*

Martin Luther

🕯 *The inner voice of God does not argue; it does not try to convince you. It just speaks, and it is self-authenticating.*

E. Stanley Jones

🕯 *The more complicated life becomes, the more we need to quiet our souls before God.*

Elisabeth Elliot

Sat

BEYOND ANGER

Wise men turn away wrath.

Proverbs 29:8 NKJV

🕉 Your temper is either your master or your servant. Either you control it, or it controls you. And the extent to which you allow anger to rule your life will determine, to a surprising extent, the quality of your relationships with others *and* your relationship with God.

Anger and peace cannot coexist in the same mind. If you allow yourself to be chronically angry, you must forfeit, albeit temporarily, the peace that might otherwise be yours through Christ. So obey God's Word by turning away from anger today and every day. You'll be glad you did, and so will your family and friends.

🕉 *For every minute you remain angry, you give up sixty seconds of peace of mind.*

Ralph Waldo Emerson

🕉 *Anger is the noise of the soul; the unseen irritant of the heart; the relentless invader of silence.*

Max Lucado

🕉 *Get rid of the poison of built-up anger and the acid of long-term resentment.*

Charles Swindoll

THE POSSESSIONS WE OWN, AND VICE VERSA

We brought nothing into the world, so we can take nothing out. But, if we have food and clothes, we will be satisfied with that.

1 Timothy 6:7, 8 NCV

🕉 How important are your material possessions? Not as important as you might think. In the life of a committed Christian, material possessions should play a rather small role. In fact, when we become overly enamored with the things we own, we needlessly distance ourselves from the peace that God offers to those who place Him at the center of their lives.

Of course, we all need the basic necessities of life, but once we meet those needs for ourselves and for our families, the piling up of possessions creates more problems than it solves. Our real riches, of course, are not of this world. We are never really rich until we are rich in spirit.

Do you find yourself wrapped up in the concerns of the material world? If so, it's time to reorder your priorities by turning your thoughts and your prayers to more important matters. And, it's time to begin storing up riches that will endure throughout eternity: the spiritual kind.

🕉 *Order your soul; reduce your wants; associate in Christian community; obey the laws; trust in Providence.*

Augustine of Hippo

mor

DIRECTING OUR THOUGHTS

Finally, brethren, whatever things are true,
whatever things are noble, whatever things are just,
whatever things are pure, whatever things are lovely,
whatever things are of good report, if there is
any virtue and if there is anything praiseworthy—
meditate on these things.

Philippians 4:8 NKJV

How will you direct your thoughts today? Will you obey the words of Philippians 4:8 by dwelling upon those things that are honorable, true, and worthy of praise? Or will you allow your thoughts to be hijacked by the negativity that seems to dominate our troubled world.

Are you fearful, angry, bored, or worried? Are you so preoccupied with the concerns of this day that you fail to thank God for the promise of eternity? Are you confused, bitter, or pessimistic? If so, God wants to have a little talk with you. He wants to remind you of His infinite love and His boundless grace. As you contemplate these things, and as you give thanks for God's blessings, negativity should no longer dominate your day *or* your life.

Certain thoughts are prayers. There are moments when, whatever be the attitude of the body, the soul is on its knees.

Victor Hugo

GIVING GOD
OUR COMPLETE ATTENTION

*For it is written, "You shall worship the Lord
your God, and Him only you shall serve."*

Matthew 4:10 NKJV

🕭 19th century clergyman Edwin Hubbel Chapin warned, "Neutral men are the devil's allies." His words were true then, and they're true now. Neutrality in the face of evil is a sin. Yet all too often, we fail to fight evil, not because we are neutral, but because we are shortsighted: We don't fight the devil because we don't recognize his handiwork.

If we are to recognize evil and fight it, we must pay careful attention. We must pay attention to God's Word, and we must pay attention to the realities of everyday life. When we observe life objectively, and when we do so with eyes and hearts that are attuned to God's Holy Word, we can no longer be neutral believers. And when we are no longer neutral, God rejoices while the devil despairs.

🕭 *Be half a Christian, and you will have just enough religion to make you miserable.*

C. H. Spurgeon

🕭 *The greatest enemy of holiness is not passion; it is apathy.*

John Eldredge

Wed

LESSONS IN PATIENCE

Therefore humble yourselves under the mighty hand of God, that He may exalt you in due time.

1 Peter 5:6 NKJV

🕊 Are you anxious for God to work out His plan for your life? Who isn't? As believers, we all want God to do great things for us and through us, and we want Him to do those things now. But sometimes, God has other plans. Sometimes, God's timetable does not coincide with our own. It's worth noting, however, that God's timetable is always perfect.

The next time you find your patience tested to the limit, remember that the world unfolds according to God's plan, not ours. Sometimes, we must wait patiently, and that's as it should be. After all, think how patient God has been with us.

🕊 *You're in a hurry. God is not. Trust God.*

Marie T. Freeman

🕊 *To wait upon God is the perfection of activity.*

Oswald Chambers

🕊 *Waiting is the hardest kind of work, but God knows best, and we may joyfully leave all in His hands.*

Lottie Moon

PETITIONING A LOVING FATHER

*Your Father knows the things you have need
of before you ask Him.*

Matthew 6:8 NKJV

🕭 Sometimes, amid the demands and the frustrations of everyday life, we forget to slow ourselves down long enough to talk with God. Instead of turning our thoughts and prayers to Him, we rely instead upon our own resources. Instead of praying for strength and courage, we seek to manufacture it within ourselves. Instead of asking God for guidance, we depend only upon our own limited wisdom. The results of such behaviors are unfortunate and, on occasion, tragic.

Are you in need? Ask God to sustain you. Are you troubled? Take your worries to Him in prayer. Are you weary? Seek God's strength. In all things great and small, seek God's wisdom and His grace. He hears your prayers, and He will answer. All you must do is ask.

🕭 *There is a communion with God that asks for nothing, yet asks for everything . . . He who seeks the Father more than anything he can give is likely to have what he asks, for he is not likely to ask amiss.*

George MacDonald

🕭 *God uses our most stumbling, faltering faith-steps as the open door to His doing for us "more than we ask or think."*

Catherine Marshall

ALONE WITH GOD

Be still, and know that I am God.

Psalm 46:10 NKJV

❧ Each day, we should spend time alone with God. But the demands of everyday living often conspire to rob us of those precious moments with our Creator. The cycle is predictable: We become so busy with the inevitable distractions of life that we fail to carve out quiet moments with our Creator. And when we do, we suffer because of our misuse of time.

We live in a world filled to overflowing with distractions, temptations, frustrations, and obligations. Our need for God is great. We must consult Him often, and we should consult Him in solitude. No time is more valuable than the quiet time we spend with God.

❧ *Ten minutes spent in Christ's society every day, aye two minutes, will make the whole day different.*

Henry Drummond

❧ *The moment you wake up each morning, all your wishes and hopes for the day rush at you like wild animals. And the first job each morning consists in shoving it all back; in listening to that other voice, taking that other point of view, letting that other, larger, stronger, quieter life coming flowing in.*

C. S. Lewis

RENEWAL DAY BY DAY

*Therefore we do not lose heart. Even though
our outward man is perishing, yet the inward man
is being renewed day by day.*

2 Corinthians 4:16 NKJV

🕀 For busy people living in a fast-paced 21st century world, life may seem like a merry-go-round that never stops turning. If that description seems to fit your life, then you may find yourself running short of patience, or strength, or both. If you're feeling tired or discouraged, there is a source from which you can draw the power needed to renew your spirit and your strength. That source is God.

🕀 *Father, for this day, renew within me the gift of the Holy Spirit.*

Andrew Murray

🕀 *Jesus is calling the weary to rest, Calling today, calling today, Bring Him your burden and you shall be blest; He will not turn you away.*

Fanny Crosby

🕀 *Walking with God leads to receiving his intimate counsel, and counseling leads to deep restoration.*

John Eldredge

Sun

THE HEART OF A THANKFUL CHRISTIAN

*In everything give thanks;
for this is the will of God in Christ Jesus for you.*

2 Thessalonians 5:18 NKJV

As believing Christians, we are blessed beyond measure. God sent his only Son to die for our sins. And, God has given us the priceless gifts of eternal love and eternal life. We, in turn, are instructed to approach our Heavenly Father with reverence and thanksgiving. But sometimes, in the crush of everyday living, we simply don't stop long enough to pause and thank our Creator for the countless blessings He has bestowed upon us.

When we slow down and express our gratitude to the One who made us, we enrich our own lives *and* the lives of those around us. Thanksgiving should become a habit, a regular part of our daily routines. God has blessed us beyond measure, and we owe Him everything, including our eternal praise. To paraphrase the familiar children's blessing, "God is great, God is good, let us thank Him for…everything!"

Words fail to express my love for this holy Book, my gratitude for its author, for His love and goodness. How shall I thank him for it?

Lottie Moon

WISDOM FROM ABOVE

*The Lord says, "I will make you wise and show you
where to go. I will guide you and watch over you."*

Psalms 32:8 NCV

🕭 From time to time, all of us encounter circumstances that test our faith. When we encounter
life's inevitable tragedies, trials, and disappointments, we may be tempted to blame God or to
rebel against Him. But the trials of life have much
to teach us, and so does God.

Have you recently encountered one of life's
inevitable tests? If so, remember that God still
has lessons that He intends to teach you. So ask
yourself this question: "What lesson is God trying
to teach me today?"

🕭 *God gives us always strength enough, and sense
enough, for everything he wants us to do.*

John Ruskin

🕭 *Knowledge is horizontal. Wisdom is vertical; it
comes down from above.*

Billy Graham

🕭 *Knowledge can be found in books or in school.
Wisdom, on the other hand, starts with God . . . and
ends there.*

Marie T. Freeman

CONTAGIOUS CHRISTIANITY

_All those who stand before others
and say they believe in me, I will say before
my Father in heaven that they belong to me._

Matthew 10:32 NCV

🕭 Genuine, heartfelt Christianity is contagious. If you enjoy a life-altering relationship with God, that relationship will have an impact on others— perhaps a profound impact.

Are you genuinely excited about your faith? And do you make your enthusiasm known to those around you? Or are you a "silent ambassador" for Christ? God's preference is clear: He intends that you stand before others and proclaim your faith.

Does Christ reign over your life? Then share your testimony _and_ your excitement. The world needs both.

🕭 _In their heart of hearts, I think all true followers of Christ long to become contagious Christians. Though unsure about how to do so or the risks involved, deep down they sense that there isn't anything as rewarding as opening a person up to God's love and truth._

Bill Hybels

🕭 _Choose Jesus Christ! Deny yourself, take up the Cross, and follow Him—for the world must be shown. The world must see, in us, a discernible, visible, startling difference._

Elisabeth Elliot

ABANDONING THE STATUS QUO

I have come as a light into the world, that whoever believes in Me should not abide in darkness.

John 12:46 NKJV

❧ It has been said that a rut is nothing more than a grave with both ends kicked out. That's a thought worth pondering. Have you made your life an exciting adventure, or have you allowed the distractions of everyday life to rob you of a sense of God's purpose?

As a believing Christian, you have every reason to celebrate. So if you find yourself feeling as if you're stuck in a rut, or in an unfortunate circumstance, or in a difficult relationship, abandon the status quo by making the changes that your heart tells you are right. After all, in God's glorious kingdom, there should be no place for disciples who are dejected, discouraged, or disheartened. God has a far better plan than that, and so should you.

❧ *True will power and courage are not on the battlefield, but in everyday conquests over our inertia, laziness, and boredom.*

D. L. Moody

❧ *Let us live with urgency. Let us exploit the opportunity of life. Let us not drift. Let us live intentionally. We must not trifle our lives away.*

Raymond Ortlund

BARNABAS,
THE ENCOURAGING FRIEND

Joseph, a Levite from Cyrus, whom the apostles called
Barnabas (which means Son of Encouragement)…

Acts 4:36 NKJV

Ɉ Barnabas, a man whose name meant "Son of Encouragement," was a leader in the early Christian church. He was known for his kindness and for his ability to encourage others. Because of Barnabas, many people were introduced to Christ. And today, as believers living in a difficult world, we must seek to imitate the "Son of Encouragement."

We imitate Barnabas when we speak kind words to our families and to our friends. We imitate Barnabas when our actions give credence to our beliefs. We imitate Barnabas when we are generous with our possessions and with our praise. We imitate Barnabas when we give hope to the hopeless and encouragement to the downtrodden.

Today, be like Barnabas: Become a source of encouragement to those who cross your path. When you do so, you will quite literally change the world, one person—and one moment—at a time.

Ɉ *Those who keep speaking about the sun while walking under a cloudy sky are messengers of hope, the true saints of our day.*

Henri J. Nouwen

Fri

VIGILANT CHRISTIANITY

*Be sober, be vigilant; because your adversary
the devil walks about like a roaring lion,
seeking whom he may devour.*

1 Peter 5:8 NKJV

🕉 Because our world is filled with temptations, we confront them at every turn. Some of these temptations are small—eating a second piece of chocolate cake, for example. Too much cake may cause us to defile, at least in a modest way, the bodily temple that God has entrusted to our care. But two pieces of cake will not bring us to our knees. Other temptations, however, are not so harmless.

The devil is hard at work in these difficult days, and as Christians we must remain vigilant. Not only must we resist Satan when he confronts us, but we must also avoid those places where Satan can most easily tempt us. And, we must earnestly wrap ourselves in the protection of God's Holy Word. When we do, we are secure.

🕉 *Arm yourself like against the devil's assaults.*

Thomas à Kempis

🕉 *Take the name of Jesus with you, as a shield from every snare; if temptations round you gather, breathe that holy name in prayer.*

Lydia Baxter

A WORLD FULL OF PROMISES

For whatever is born of God overcomes the world.
And this is the victory
that has overcome the world—our faith.

1 John 5:4 NKJV

🔥 The world makes promises that it simply cannot fulfill. It promises happiness, contentment, prosperity, and abundance. But genuine, lasting abundance is not a function of worldly possessions, it is a function of our thoughts, our actions, and the relationship we choose to create with our God. The world's promises are incomplete and illusory; God's promises are unfailing.

We must build our lives on the firm foundation of God's promises . . . nothing else will suffice.

🔥 *Nothing is more foolish than a security built upon the world and its promises, for they are all vanity and a lie.*

Matthew Henry

🔥 *The true Christian, though he is in revolt against the world's efforts to brainwash him, is no mere rebel for rebellion's sake. He dissents from the world because he knows that it cannot make good on its promises.*

A. W. Tozer

OBEDIENCE TO THE ULTIMATE AUTHORITY

But Peter and the other apostles answered and said:
"We ought to obey God rather than men."

Acts 5:29 NKJV

❧ Obedience to God is determined, not by words, but by deeds. Talking about righteousness is easy; living righteously is far more difficult, especially in today's fast-paced, temptation-filled world. Since God created Adam and Eve, we human beings have been rebelling against our Creator. Why? Because we are unwilling to trust God's Word, and we are unwilling to follow His commandments. God has given us a guidebook for righteous living called the Holy Bible. It contains thorough instructions which, if followed, lead to fulfillment, righteousness and salvation. But, if we choose to ignore God's commandments, the results are as predictable as they are tragic.

Unless we are willing to abide by God's laws, all of our righteous proclamations ring hollow. How can we best proclaim our love for the Lord? By obeying Him. And, for further instructions, read the manual.

❧ *Give me, good Lord, such a love for You that I will love nothing in a way that displeases You, and I will love everything for Your sake.*

Thomas More

Mon

GUIDED BY HONESTY

Good people will be guided by honesty;
dishonesty will destroy those who are not trustworthy.

Proverbs 11:3 NCV

❧ Charles Swindoll correctly observed, "Nothing speaks louder or more powerfully than a life of integrity." Godly men and women agree.

Integrity is built slowly over a lifetime. It is a precious thing—difficult to build but easy to tear down. As believers in Christ, we must seek to live each day with discipline, honesty, and faith. When we do, at least two things happen: Integrity becomes a habit, and God blesses us because of our obedience to Him.

Living a life of integrity isn't always the easiest way, but it is always right way. And God clearly intends that it should be our way, too.

❧ *Lying covers a multitude of sins—temporarily.*

D. L. Moody

❧ *Honest men fear neither the light nor the dark.*

Thomas Fuller

❧ *God never called us to naïveté. He called us to integrity.... The biblical concept of integrity emphasizes mature innocence not childlike ignorance.*

Beth Moore

SINCE TOMORROW IS NOT PROMISED

I must work the works of Him who sent Me
while it is day; the night is coming
when no one can work.

John 9:4 NKJV

🕯 The words of John 9:4 remind us that "night is coming" for all of us. But until then, God gives us each day and fills it to the brim with possibilities. The day is presented to us fresh and clean at midnight, free of charge, but we must beware: Today is a non-renewable resource—once it's gone, it's gone forever. Our responsibility, of course, is to use this day in the service of God's will and in accordance with His commandments.

Today, treasure the time that God has given you. And search for the hidden possibilities that God has placed along your path. This day is a priceless gift from your Creator, so use it joyfully and productively. And encourage others to do likewise.

🕯 *Live in such a way that any day would make a suitable capstone for life. Live so that you need not change your mode of living, even if your sudden departure were immediately predicted to you.*

C. H. Spurgeon

Wed

THE RICH HARVEST

But this I say: He who sows sparingly will also reap sparingly, and he who sows bountifully will also reap bountifully.

2 Corinthians 9:6 NKJV

🌸 How can we serve God? By sharing His message, His mercy, and His love with those who cross our paths. Everywhere we look, or so it seems, the needs are great. And at every turn, it seems, so are the temptations. Still, our challenge is clear: We must love God, obey His commandments, trust His Son, and serve His children. When we place the Lord in His rightful place—at the center of our lives—we will reap a bountiful spiritual harvest that will endure forever.

🌸 *An idle life and a holy heart are a contradiction.*

Thomas Brooks

🌸 *That's what I love about serving God. In His eyes, there are no little people . . . because there are no big people. We are all on the same playing field.*

Joni Eareckson Tada

🌸 *Discipleship means personal, passionate devotion to a Person, our Lord Jesus Christ.*

Oswald Chambers

QUIET, PLEASE!

Truly my soul silently waits for God;
from Him comes my salvation.

Psalms 62:1 NKJV

🐚 The world seems to grow louder day by day, and our senses seem to be invaded at every turn. If we allow the distractions of a clamorous society to separate us from God's peace, we do ourselves a profound disservice. Our task, as dutiful believers, is to carve out moments of silence in a world filled with noise.

If we are to maintain righteous minds and compassionate hearts, we must take time each day for prayer and for meditation. We must make ourselves still in the presence of our Creator. We must quiet our minds and our hearts so that we might sense God's will and His love.

Has the busy pace of life robbed you of the peace that God has promised? If so, it's time to reorder your priorities and your life. Nothing is more important than the time you spend with your Heavenly Father. So be still and claim the inner peace that is found in the silent moments you spend with God.

🐚 *The remedy for distractions is the same now as it was in earlier and simpler times: prayer, meditation, and the cultivation of the inner life.*

A. W. Tozer

SELECTING YOUR ROADMAP

Teach me, O Lord, the way of Your statutes,
and I shall keep it to the end.

Psalms 119:33 NKJV

🕉 As you look to the future and decide upon the direction of your life, what will you use as your roadmap? Will you trust God's Holy Word and use it as an indispensable tool to guide your steps? Or will you choose a different map to guide your steps? The map you choose will determine the quality of your journey *and* its ultimate destination.

The Bible is the ultimate guide for life; make it your guidebook as well. When you do, you can be comforted in the knowledge that your steps are guided by a Source of wisdom and truth that never fails.

🕉 *He who is his own guide is guided by a fool.*

C. H. Spurgeon

🕉 *Some read the Bible to learn and some read the Bible to hear from heaven.*

Andrew Murray

🕉 *The Bible was not given to increase our knowledge but to change our lives.*

D. L. Moody

STEWARDSHIP OF YOUR TIME

So teach us to number our days,
that we may gain a heart of wisdom.

Psalm 90:12 NKJV

🕊 Time is a nonrenewable gift from God. But sometimes, we treat our time here on earth as if it were not a gift at all: We may be tempted to invest our lives in trivial pursuits and petty diversions. But our Father beckons each of us to a higher calling.

An important element of our stewardship to God is the way that we choose to spend the time He has entrusted to us. Each waking moment holds the potential to do a good deed, to say a kind word, or to offer a heartfelt prayer. Our challenge, as believers, is use our time wisely in the service of God's work and in accordance with His plan for our lives.

Each day is a special treasure to be savored and celebrated. May we—as Christians who have so much to celebrate—never fail to praise our Creator by rejoicing in this glorious day, and by using it wisely.

🕊 *Our leisure, even our play, is a matter of serious concern. There is no neutral ground in the universe: every square inch, every split second, is claimed by God and counterclaimed by Satan.*

C. S. Lewis

A GOD OF POSSIBILITIES

But Jesus looked at them and said to them,
"With men this is impossible,
but with God all things are possible."

Matthew 19:26 NKJV

All of mankind is engaged in worship…of one kind or another. The question is not *whether* we worship, but *what* we worship. Some of us choose to worship God. The result is a plentiful harvest of joy, peace, and abundance. Others distance themselves from God by foolishly worshiping things of this earth such as fame, fortune, or personal gratification. To do so is a terrible mistake with eternal consequences.

How can we ensure that we cast our lot with God? We do so, in part, by the practice of regular, purposeful worship in the company of fellow believers. When we worship God faithfully and fervently, we are blessed. When we fail to worship God, for whatever reason, we forfeit the spiritual gifts that He intends for us to have.

We must worship our heavenly Father, not just with our words, but also with deeds. We must honor Him, praise Him, and obey Him. As we seek to find purpose and meaning for our lives, we must first seek *His* purpose and *His* will. For believers, God comes first. Always first.

The fact that we were created to enjoy God and to worship him forever is etched upon our souls.

Jim Cymbala

THE REWARDS OF RIGHTEOUSNESS

Test all things; hold fast what is good.
Abstain from every form of evil.
1 Thessalonians 5:21, 22 NKJV

❧ When we seek righteousness in our own lives—
and when we seek the companionship of those
who do likewise—we reap the spiritual rewards
that God intends for us to enjoy. When we behave
ourselves as godly men and women, we honor God.
When we live righteously and according to God's
commandments, He blesses us in ways that we
cannot fully understand.

Today, as you fulfill your responsibilities, hold
fast that which is good, and associate yourself
with believers who behave themselves in like
fashion. When you do, your good works will serve
as a powerful example for others *and* as a worthy
offering to your Creator.

❧ *I don't care what a man says he believes with his lips.*
I want to know with a vengeance what he says with his
life and his actions.

Sam Jones

❧ *The holier a man becomes, the more he mourns the*
unholiness that remains in him.

C. H. Spurgeon

❧ *Trusting God is the bottom line of Christian*
righteousness.

R. C. Sproul

PRAYERFUL HEARTS AND WILLING HANDS

So you may walk in the way of goodness, and keep to the paths of righteousness. For the upright will dwell in the land, and the blameless will remain in it.

Proverbs 2:20, 21 NKJV

🐟 The old adage is both familiar and true: We must pray as if everything depended upon God, but work as if everything depended upon us. Yet sometimes, when we are weary and discouraged, we may allow our worries to sap our energy and our hope. God has other intentions. God intends that we pray for things, *and* He intends that we be willing to work for the things that we pray for. More importantly, God intends that *our* work should become *His* work.

Are you willing to work diligently for yourself, for your family, and for your God? And are you willing to engage in work that is pleasing to your Creator? If so, you can expect your Heavenly Father to bring forth a rich harvest.

And if you have concerns about the inevitable challenges of everyday living, take those concerns to God in prayer. He will guide your steps, He will steady your hand, He will calm your fears, and He will reward your efforts.

🐟 *The things, good Lord, that I pray for, give me the grace to labor for.*

Thomas More

QUIET CHARITY

Take heed that you do not do your charitable deeds
before men, to be seen by them.
Otherwise you have no reward in heaven.

Matthew 6:1 NKJV

❧ Hymn writer Fanny Crosby wrote, "To God be the glory; great things He hath done!" But sometimes, because we are imperfect human beings, we seek the glory. Sometimes, when we do good deeds, we seek to glorify our achievements in a vain attempt build ourselves up in the eyes of our neighbors. To do so is a profound mistake.

God's Word gives specific instructions about how we should approach our acts of charity: The glory must go to God, not to us. All praise belongs to the Giver of all good gifts: our Father in Heaven. We are simply conduits for His generosity, and we must remain humble . . . *extremely* humble.

❧ *We must be charitable, and humble, and give alms because charity washes the stains of sin from our souls.*

St. Francis of Assisi

❧ *All kindness and good deeds, we must keep silent. The result will be an inner reservoir of power.*

Catherine Marshall

CONCERNING THE LOVE OF MONEY

Keep your lives free from the love of money,
and be satisfied with what you have.

Hebrews 13:5 NCV

🕉 In our modern society, we need money to live. But as Christians, we must never make the acquisition of money the central focus of our lives. Money is a tool, but it should never overwhelm our sensibilities. The focus of life must be squarely on things spiritual, not things material.

Whenever we place our love for material possessions above our love for God—or when we yield to the countless other temptations of everyday living—we find ourselves engaged in a struggle between good and evil, a clash between God and Satan. Our responses to these struggles have implications that echo throughout our families and throughout our communities. Let us choose wisely by freeing ourselves from that subtle yet powerful temptation: the temptation to love the world more than we love God.

🕉 *Many things I have tried to grasp and have lost. That which I have placed in God's hands I still have.*

Martin Luther

🕉 *Servants of God are always more concerned about ministry than money.*

Rick Warren

THE SEARCH FOR WISDOM

If any of you lacks wisdom, let him ask of God,
who gives to all liberally and without reproach,
and it will be given to him.

James 1:5 NKJV

❧ Do you seek the wisdom that only God can give? If so, ask Him for it! If you ask God for guidance, He will not withhold it. If you petition Him sincerely, and if you genuinely seek to form a relationship with Him, your Heavenly Father will guide your steps and enlighten your heart. But be forewarned: You will not acquire God's wisdom without obeying His commandments. Why? Because God's wisdom is more than just a collection of thoughts; it is, first and foremost, a way of life.

Wisdom is as wisdom does. So if you sincerely seek God's wisdom, don't be satisfied to *learn* something; make up your mind to *become* something. And then, as you allow God to remake you in the image of His Son, you will most surely become wise.

❧ *Ask the God who made you to keep remaking you.*

Norman Vincent Peale

❧ *Wisdom is the God-given ability to see life with rare objectivity and to handle life with rare stability.*

Charles Swindoll

Sat

GIVING AN ACCOUNT OF OURSELVES

*So then each of us shall give account
of himself to God.*

Romans 14:12 NKJV

🕉 For most of us, it is a daunting thought: One day, perhaps soon, we'll come face-to-face with our Heavenly Father, and we'll be called to account for our actions here on earth. Our personal histories will certainly *not* be surprising to God; He already knows everything about us. But the full scope of our activities *may* be surprising to us: Some of us will be pleasantly surprised; others will not be.

Today, do whatever you can to ensure that your thoughts and your deeds are pleasing to your Creator. Because you will, at some point in the future, be called to account for your actions. And the future may be sooner than you think.

🕉 *Don't worry about what you do not understand. Worry about what you do understand in the Bible but do not live by.*

Corrie ten Boom

🕉 *He who obeys not the rudder will obey the reef.*

Herve of Brittany

🕉 *In every act that we do, in every step we take, let our hand trace the Lord's Cross.*

Jerome

THE TIME TO PLANT SEEDS

*Those who wait for perfect weather will never
plant seeds; those who look at every cloud will never
harvest crops. Plant early in the morning, and work
until evening, because you don't know if this or that
will succeed. They might both do well.*

Ecclesiastes 11:4, 6 NCV

🕉 Once the season for planting is upon us, the time
to plant seeds is when we *make* time to plant seeds.
And when it comes to planting *God's* seeds in the
soil of eternity, the only certain time that we have
is now. Yet, because we are fallible human beings
with limited vision and misplaced priorities, we
may be tempted to delay.

If we hope to reap a bountiful harvest for God,
for our families, and for ourselves, we must plant
now by defeating a dreaded human frailty: the
habit of procrastination. Procrastination often
results from our shortsighted attempts to postpone
temporary discomfort.

A far better strategy is this: Whatever "it" is,
do it now. When you do, you won't have to worry
about "it" later.

🕉 *He who waits until circumstances completely favor
his undertaking will never accomplish anything.*

Martin Luther

🕉 *Do noble things, do not dream them all day long.*

Charles Kingsley

WHAT WE BELIEVE AND HOW WE BEHAVE

Not everyone who says to Me, 'Lord, Lord,'
shall enter the kingdom of heaven,
but he who does the will of My Father in heaven.

Matthew 7:21 NKJV

🕊 In describing one's beliefs, actions are far better descriptors than words. Yet far too many of us spend more energy *talking* about our beliefs than *living* by them—with predictable consequences.

Is your life a picture book of your creed? Are your actions congruent with your beliefs? Are you willing to practice the philosophy that you preach?

Today and every day, make certain that your actions are guided by God's Word and by the conscience that He has placed in your heart. Don't treat your faith as if it were separate from your everyday life. Weave your beliefs into the very fabric of your day. When you do, God will honor your good works, and your good works will honor God.

🕊 *He does not believe who does not live according to his beliefs.*

Thomas Fuller

🕊 *Understanding is the reward of faith. Therefore, seek not to understand that you may believe, but believe that you may understand.*

St. Augustine of Hippo

SPIRITUAL MATURITY, DAY BY DAY

When I was a child, I spoke as a child,
I understood as a child, I thought as a child;
but when I became a man, I put away childish things.

1 Corinthians 13:11 NKJV

✒ The path to spiritual maturity unfolds day by day. Each day offers the opportunity to worship God, to ignore God, or to rebel against God. When we worship Him with our prayers, our words, our thoughts, and our actions, we are blessed by the richness of our relationship with the Father. But if we ignore God altogether or intentionally rebel against His commandments, we rob ourselves of His blessings.

Today offers yet another opportunity for spiritual growth. If you choose, you can seize that opportunity by obeying God's Word, by seeking His will, and by walking with His Son.

✒ *Happy is he who makes daily progress and who considers not what he did yesterday but what advance he can make today.*

Jerome

✒ *We cannot hope to reach Christian maturity in any way other than by yielding ourselves utterly and willingly to His mighty working.*

Hannah Whitall Smith

BEYOND STUBBORNNESS

Pride goes before destruction,
and a haughty spirit before a fall.

Proverbs 16:18 NKJV

🕭 Since the days of Adam and Eve, human beings have been strong-willed and rebellious. Our rebellion stems, in large part, from an intense desire to do things "our way" instead of "God's way." But when we pridefully choose to forsake God's path for our lives, we do ourselves a sincere injustice . . . and we are penalized because of our stubbornness.

God's Word warns us to be humble, not prideful. God instructs us to be obedient, not rebellious. God wants us to do things His way. When we do, we reap a bountiful harvest of blessings—more blessings than we can count. But when we pridefully rebel against our Creator, we sow the seeds of our own destruction, and we reap a sad, sparse, bitter harvest. May we sow—and reap— accordingly.

🕭 *If it your goal to always be right in everything, your soul will suffer.*

Thérèse of Lisieux

🕭 *God uses broken things: broken soil and broken clouds to produce grain; broken grain to produce bread; broken bread to feed our bodies. He wants our stubbornness broken into humble obedience.*

Vance Havner

THE ART OF GODLY ACCEPTANCE

People may make plans in their minds,
but the Lord decides what they will do.

Proverbs 16:9 NCV

S Sometimes, we must accept life on its terms, not our own. Life has a way of unfolding, not as *we* will, but as *it* will. And sometimes, there is precious little we can do to change things.

When events transpire that are beyond our control, we have a choice: We can either learn the art of acceptance, or we can make ourselves miserable as we struggle to change the unchangable.

We must entrust the things we *cannot* change to God. Once we have done so, we can prayerfully and faithfully tackle the important work that He has placed before us: the things we *can* change.

S *Our Lord never asks us to decide for Him; He asks us to yield to Him—a very different matter.*

Oswald Chambers

S *God does not furnish us with a detailed road map. When we are with Him, we may not always know whither, but we know with whom.*

Vance Havner

WHEN WE DO OUR PART, GOD DOES HIS

And we know that all things work together for good to those who love God, to those who are the called according to His purpose.

Romans 8:28 NKJV

🕭 God is willing to protect us. We, in turn, must open ourselves to His protection and His love. This point is illustrated by the familiar story found in the 4th chapter of Mark: When a terrible storm rose quickly on the Sea of Galilee, the disciples were afraid. Although they had witnessed many miracles, the disciples feared for their lives, so they turned to Jesus, and He calmed the waters and the wind.

Sometimes, we, like the disciples, feel threatened by the storms of life. And when we are fearful, we, too, can turn to Christ for comfort and for courage. The next time you find yourself facing a fear-provoking situation, remember that the One who calmed the wind and the waves is also your personal Savior. Then ask yourself which is stronger: your faith or your fear. The answer, friends, should be obvious: Whatever your challenge, God can handle it. Let Him.

🕭 *Call upon God. Prayer itself can defuse fear.*

Bill Hybels

Lifetime Learning

Wisdom is the principal thing; therefore get wisdom.
And in all your getting, get understanding.

Proverbs 4:7 NKJV

✠ Whether you're twenty-two or a hundred and two, you've still got lots to learn. Even if you're a very wise person, God isn't finished with you yet. Why? Because lifetime learning is part of God's plan—and He certainly hasn't finished teaching _you_ some very important lessons.

Do you seek to live a life of righteousness and wisdom? If so, you must continue to study the ultimate source of wisdom: the Word of God. You must associate, day in and day out, with godly men and women. And, you must act in accordance with your beliefs. When you study God's Word and live according to His commandments, you will become wise . . . and you will be a blessing to your friends, to you family, and to the world.

✠ _Life is not a holiday, but an education. And the one eternal lesson for us all is how better we can love._

Henry Drummond

✠ _True learning can take place at every age of life, and it doesn't have to be in the curriculum plan._

Suzanne Dale Ezell

HABITS THAT ARE PLEASING TO GOD

I, the Lord, search the heart, I test the mind,
even to give every man according to his ways,
according to the fruit of his doings.

Jeremiah 17:10 NKJV

֍ It's an old saying and a true one: First, you make your habits, and then your habits make you. Some habits will inevitably bring you closer to God; other habits will lead you away from the path He has chosen for you. If you sincerely desire to improve your spiritual health, you must honestly examine the habits that make up the fabric of your day. And you must abandon those habits that are displeasing to God.

If you trust God, and if you keep asking for His help, He can transform your life. If you sincerely ask Him to help you, the same God who created the universe will help you defeat the harmful habits that have heretofore defeated you. So, if at first you don't succeed, keep praying. God is listening, and He's ready to help you become a better person *if* you ask Him . . . so ask today.

֍ *He who does not overcome small faults, shall fall little by little into greater ones.*

Thomas à Kempis

FOLLOWING HIS FOOTSTEPS

But whoever keeps His word, truly the love of God is perfected in him. By this we know that we are in Him. He who says he abides in Him ought himself also to walk just as He walked.

1 John 2:5, 6 NKJV

❧ Life is a series of decisions and choices. Each day, we make countless decisions that can bring us closer to God…or not. When we live according to God's commandments, we reap bountiful rewards: Abundance, hope, and peace, for starters. But, when we turn our backs upon God by disobeying Him, we bring needless suffering upon ourselves and our families.

Do you seek to walk in the footsteps of the One from Galilee, or will you choose another path? If you sincerely seek God's peace and His blessings, then you must strive to imitate God's Son.

Thomas Brooks spoke for believers of every generation when he observed, "Christ is the sun, and all the watches of our lives should be set by the dial of his motion." Christ, indeed, is the ultimate savior of mankind and the personal savior of those who believe in Him. As His servants, we should walk in His footsteps as we share His love and His message with a world that needs both.

❧ *If you are looking for the way by which you should go, take Christ, for he is himself the way.*
Thomas Aquinas

AIMING HIGH

*I can do all things through Christ
who strengthens me.*

Philippians 4:13 NKJV

❧ Are you willing to dream big dreams? Hopefully so; after all, God promises that we can do "all things" through Him. Yet most of us, even the most devout among us, live far below our potential. We take half measures; we dream small dreams; we waste precious time and energy on the distractions of the world. But God has other plans for us. Our Creator intends that we live faithfully, hopefully, courageously, and abundantly. He knows that we are capable of so much more; and He wants us to do the things we're capable of doing; and He wants us to start doing those things now.

❧ *You pay God a compliment by asking great things of Him.*

St. Teresa of Avila

❧ *The Lord Himself has laid the foundation of His people's hopes. We must determine if our hopes are built on this foundation.*

C. H. Spurgeon

❧ *You cannot out-dream God.*

John Eldredge

THE SOURCE OF STRENGTH

Blessed is the man whose strength is in You,
whose heart is set on pilgrimage.

Psalm 84:5 NKJV

Have you "tapped in" to the power of God? Have you turned your life and your heart over to Him, or are you muddling along under your own power? The answer to this question will determine the quality of your life here on earth and the destiny of your life throughout all eternity.

The Bible tells us that we can do all things through the power of our risen Savior, Jesus Christ. But what does the Bible say about our powers *outside* the will of Christ? The Bible teaches us that "the wages of sin is death" (Romans 6:23). Our challenge, then, is clear: We must place Christ where he belongs: at the very center of our lives. When we do so, we will surely discover that He offers us the strength to live victoriously in this world *and* eternally in the next.

Jesus is all the world to me, my life, my joy, my all; He is my strength from day to day, without Him I would fall.

Will L. Thompson

You are mighty, Lord, you are mighty. Nothing compares to you in power. No one can equal the strength of your hand.

Mary Morrison Suggs

THE SEARCH FOR TRUTH

And you shall know the truth,
and the truth shall make you free.

John 8:32 NKJV

🕉 The words of John 8:32 are both familiar and profound: The truth, indeed, will make you free. Truth is God's way. He commands His children to live in truth, and He rewards those who follow His commandment. Jesus is the personification of a perfect, liberating truth that offers salvation to mankind.

Do you seek to walk with God? Do you seek to feel God's peace? Then you must walk in truth, and you must walk with the Savior. There is simply no other way.

🕉 *I would rather know the truth than be happy in ignorance. If I cannot have both truth and happiness, give me truth. We'll have a long time to be happy in heaven.*

A. W. Tozer

🕉 *The Holy Spirit was given to guide us into all truth, but He doesn't do it all at once.*

Elisabeth Elliot

🕉 *Let everything perish! Dismiss these empty vanities! And let us take up the search for the truth.*

St. Augustine of Hippo

Encouraging Words for Family and Friends

Good people's words will help many others.

Proverbs 10:21 NCV

❧ Life is a team sport, and all of us need occasional pats on the back from our teammates. As Christians, we are called upon to spread the Good News of Christ, and we are also called to spread a message of encouragement and hope to the world.

Whether you realize it or not, many people with whom you come in contact every day are in desperate need of a smile or an encouraging word. The world can be a difficult place, and countless friends and family members may be troubled by the challenges of everyday life. Since you don't always know who needs our help, the best strategy is to try to encourage *all* the people who cross your path. So today, be a world-class source of encouragement to everyone you meet. Never has the need been greater.

❧ *Encouragement starts at home, but it should never end there.*

Marie T. Freeman

❧ *Happiness is to be found only in the home where God is loved and honored, where each one loves, and helps, and cares for the others.*

Theophane Venard

KEEPING PROSPERITY IN PERSPECTIVE

If riches increase, do not set your heart on them.

Psalm 62:10 NKJV

❖ In the demanding world in which we live, financial prosperity can be a good thing, but *spiritual* prosperity is profoundly more important. Yet our society leads us to believe otherwise. The world glorifies material possessions, personal fame, and physical beauty above all else; these things are totally unimportant to God. God sees the human heart, and that's what is important to Him.

As you establish your priorities for the coming day, remember this: The world will do everything it can to convince you that "things" are important. The world will tempt you to value fortune above faith and possessions above peace. God, on the other hand, will try to convince you that your relationship with Him is all-important. Trust God.

❖ *Have you prayed about your resources lately? Find out how God wants you to use your time and your money. No matter what it costs, forsake all that is not of God.*

Kay Arthur

❖ *Prosperity is not without many fears and distastes; adversity not without many comforts and hopes.*

Francis Bacon

FINDING PURPOSE
THROUGH CHARITY

Happy is the person who thinks about the poor.
When trouble comes, the Lord will save him.

Psalms 41:1 NCV

🕕 God's Words commands us to be generous, compassionate servants to those who need our support. As believers, we have been richly blessed by our Creator. We, in turn, are called to share our gifts, our possessions, our testimonies, and our talents.

Concentration camp survivor Corrie ten Boom correctly observed, "The measure of a life is not its duration but its donation." These words remind us that the quality of our lives is determined not by what are able to take *from* others, but instead by what we are able to share *with* others.

The thread of generosity is woven into the very fabric of Christ's teachings. If we are to be His disciples, then we, too, must be cheerful, generous, courageous givers. Our Savior expects no less from us. And He deserves no less.

🕕 *Selfishness is as far from Christianity as darkness is from light.*

C. H. Spurgeon

🕕 *Did universal charity prevail, earth would be a heaven and hell a fable.*

Charles Caleb Colton

THE WISDOM OF RIGHTEOUSNESS

To do evil is like sport to a fool,
but a man of understanding has wisdom.

Proverbs 10:23 NKJV

🕉 Everyday life is an adventure in decision-making. Each day, we make countless decisions that hopefully bring us closer to God. When we live according to God's commandments, we share in His abundance and His peace. But, when we turn our backs upon God by disobeying Him, we bring needless suffering upon ourselves and upon our families.

Do you seek God's peace and His blessings? Then obey Him. When you're faced with a difficult choice or a powerful temptation, seek God's counsel and trust the counsel He gives. Invite God into your heart and live according to His commandments. When you do, you will be blessed today, and tomorrow, and forever.

🕉 *The power of choosing good and evil is within the reach of all.*

Origen of Alexandria

🕉 *Sanctify yourself and you will sanctify society.*

Francis of Assisi

FINDING YOUR WAY

*In all your ways acknowledge Him,
and He shall direct your paths.*

Proverbs 3:6 NKJV

❧ Proverbs 3:6 makes this promise: If you acknowledge God's sovereignty over every aspect of your life, He will guide your path. And, as prayerfully consider the path that God intends for you to take, here are things you should do: You should study His Word and be ever-watchful for His signs. You should associate with fellow believers who will encourage your spiritual growth. You should listen carefully to that inner voice that speaks to you in the quiet moments of your daily devotionals. And, as you continually seek God's unfolding purpose for your life, you should be patient. Your Heavenly Father may not always reveal himself as quickly as you would like. But rest assured: God is here, and He intends to use you in wonderful, unexpected ways. He desires to lead you along a path of His choosing. Your challenge is to watch, to listen, to learn . . . and to follow.

❧ *When you discover the Christian way, you discover your own way as a person.*

E. Stanley Jones

❧ *There is a path before you that you alone can walk. There is a purpose that you alone can fulfill.*

Karla Dornacher

When We Stumble

God is our refuge and strength,
a very present help in trouble.

Psalm 46:1 NKJV

From time to time, all of us face adversity, discouragement, or disappointment. And, throughout life, we must all endure life-changing personal losses that leave us breathless. When we do, God stands ready to protect us. Psalm 147 promises, "He heals the brokenhearted and bandages their wounds" (v. 3, NCV).

When we are troubled, we must call upon God, and, in His own time and according to His own plan, He will heal us.

Are you anxious? Take those anxieties to God. Are you troubled? Take your troubles to Him. Does your world seem to be trembling beneath your feet? Seek protection from the One who cannot be moved. The same God who created the universe will protect you if you ask Him...so ask Him.

Measure the size of the obstacles against the size of God.

Beth Moore

We all go through pain and sorrow, but the presence of God, like a warm, comforting blanket, can shield us and protect us, and allow the deep inner joy to surface, even in the most devastating circumstances.

Barbara Johnson

EARTHLY STRESS, HEAVENLY PEACE

And let the peace of God rule in your hearts, to which also you were called in one body; and be thankful.

Colossians 3:15 NKJV

  Stressful days are an inevitable fact of life. And how do we best cope with the challenges of our demanding, 21st-century world? By turning our days and our lives over to God. Elisabeth Elliot writes, "If my life is surrendered to God, all is well. Let me not grab it back, as though it were in peril in His hand but would be safer in mine!" Yet even the most devout Christian woman may, at times, seek to grab the reins of her life and proclaim, "I'm in charge!" To do so is foolish, prideful, and stressful.

Do you feel overwhelmed by the stresses of daily life? Turn your concerns and your prayers over to God. Trust Him completely. Trust Him today. Trust Him always. When it comes to the inevitable challenges of this day, hand them over to God completely and without reservation. He knows your needs and will meet those needs in His own way and in His own time if you let Him.

  God knows what each of us is dealing with. He knows our pressures. He knows our conflicts. And, He has made a provision for each and every one of them. That provision is Himself in the person of the Holy Spirit, dwelling in us and empowering us to respond rightly.

Kay Arthur

FEARING GOD,
HUMBLING OURSELVES

Respecting the Lord and not being proud
will bring you wealth, honor, and life.

Proverbs 22:4 NCV

&. Do you have a healthy, fearful respect for God's power? If so, you are both wise *and* obedient. And, because you are a thoughtful believer, you also understand that genuine wisdom begins with a profound appreciation for God's limitless power.

God praises humility and punishes pride. That's why God's greatest servants will always be those humble men and women who care less for their own glory and more for God's glory. In God's kingdom, the only way to achieve greatness is to shun it. And the only way to be wise is to understand these facts: God is great; He is all-knowing; and He is all-powerful. We must respect Him, and we must humble obey His commandments, or we must accept the consequences of our misplaced pride.

&. *The source of humility is the habit of realizing the presence of God.*

William Temple

&. *Humility is not thinking less of yourself; it is thinking of yourself less.*

Rick Warren

STANDING ON THE ROCK

*Therefore whoever hears these sayings of Mine,
and does them, I will liken him to a wise man
who built his house on the rock.*

Matthew 7:24 NKJV

❧ God is the Creator of life, the Sustainer of life, and the Rock upon which righteous lives are built. God is a never-ending source of support for those who trust Him, and He is a never-ending source of wisdom for those who study His Holy Word.

Is God the Rock upon which you've constructed your own life? If so, then you have chosen wisely. Your faith will give you the inner strength you need to rise above the inevitable demands and struggles of life here on earth.

Do the demands of this day seem overwhelming? If so, you must rely not only upon your own resources, but, more importantly, upon the Rock that cannot be shaken. God will hold your hand and walk with you today and every day if you let Him. Even if your circumstances are difficult, trust the Father. His promises remain true; His love is eternal; and His goodness endures. And because He is the One who can never be moved, you can stand firm in the knowledge that you are protected by Him now and forever.

❧ *Trust in God, and you are never to be confounded in time or eternity.*

D. L. Moody

PRAISE AND CRITICISM

*Our only goal is to please God whether we live
here or there, because we must all
stand before Christ to be judged.*

2 Corinthians 5:9, 10 NCV

&o If you're like most people, you seek the admiration of your neighbors, your coworkers, and your family members. But the eagerness to please others should never overshadow your eagerness to please God. In every aspect of your life, pleasing your Heavenly Father should come first.

Would you like a time-tested formula for successful living? Here is a formula that is proven and true: Seek God's approval *first* and other people's approval later. Does this sound too simple? Perhaps it is simple, but it is also the only way to reap the marvelous riches that God has in store for you.

&o *It is comfortable to know that we are responsible to God and not to man. It is a small matter to be judged of man's judgement.*

Lottie Moon

&o *When we are set free from the bondage of pleasing others, when we are free from currying others' favor and others' approval—then no one will be able to make us miserable or dissatisfied. And then, if we know we have pleased God, contentment will be our consolation.*

Kay Arthur

THE ULTIMATE PARTNER

For we are God's fellow workers; you are God's field,
you are God's building.

1 Corinthians 3:9 NKJV

&o If you want to be successful—genuinely successful in the things that really matter—you need a partner. That Partner is God. And the good news is this: When you humbly and sincerely ask God to become your partner, He will grant your request and transform your life.

Is your life a testimony to the personal relationship that you enjoy with your Heavenly Father? Or have you compartmentalized your faith to a few hours on Sunday morning? If you genuinely wish to make God your fulltime partner, you must allow Him to reign over every aspect of your life and every day of your week. When you do, you'll be amazed at the things that the two of you, working together, can accomplish.

&o *We do the works, but God works in us in the doing of the works.*

St. Augustine of Hippo

&o *Help yourself and God will help you.*

Joan of Arc

&o *God's never been guilty of sponsoring a flop.*

Ethel Waters

GOD IS PERFECT; WE ARE NOT

For all have sinned and fall short of the glory of God.
Romans 3:23 NKJV

Expectations, expectations, expectations! The media delivers an endless stream of messages that tell you how to look, how to behave, and how to dress. The media's expectations are impossible to meet—God's are not. God doesn't expect perfection . . . and neither should you.

If you find yourself bound up by the chains of perfectionism, it's time to ask yourself who you're trying to impress, and why. If you're trying to impress other people, it's time to reconsider your priorities. Your first responsibility is to the heavenly Father who created you and to His Son who saved you. Then, you bear a powerful responsibility to your family. But, when it comes to meeting society's unrealistic expectations, forget it!

Remember that when you accepted Christ as your Savior, God accepted you for all eternity. Now, it's your turn to accept yourself and your loved ones. When you do, you'll feel a tremendous weight being lifted from your shoulders. After all, pleasing God is simply a matter of obeying His commandments and accepting His Son. But as for pleasing everybody else? That's impossible!

The happiest people in the world are not those who have no problems, but the people who have learned to live with those things that are less than perfect.
James Dobson

APART FROM THE WORLD

Do not love the world or the things in the world.
If anyone loves the world,
the love of the Father is not in him.

1 John 2:15 NKJV

❧ We live in the world, but we must not worship it. Our duty is to place God first and everything else second. But because we are fallible beings with imperfect faith, placing God in His rightful place is often difficult. In fact, at every turn, or so it seems, we are tempted to do otherwise.

The 21st-Century world is a noisy, distracting place filled with countless opportunities to stray from God's will. The world seems to cry, "Worship me with your time, your money, your energy, and your thoughts!" But God commands otherwise: He commands us to worship Him and Him alone; everything else must be secondary.

❧ *Our joy ends where love of the world begins.*

C. H. Spurgeon

❧ *Don't have Jesus Christ on your lips and the world in your hearts.*

Ignatius of Antioch

❧ *You will feel that he must rule and control each day. My prayer, my faith, my fellowship with the Father, and all my work in God's service, must be completely under His sway.*

Andrew Murray

Persistent Prayer

Watch therefore, and pray always. . . .

Luke 21:36 NKJV

&⁊ When we weave the habit of prayer into the very fabric of our days, we invite God to become a full partner in every aspect of our lives. When we consult God on an hourly basis, we avail ourselves of His wisdom, His strength, and His love. When we pray constantly about things great and small, we receive answers that direct our steps and lift our spirits.

Today, as you meet the challenges of everyday life, pray about every aspect of your life. God is always here, and He has answers that *you* need to hear.

&⁊ *Jesus taught that perseverance is the essential element in prayer.*

E. M. Bounds

&⁊ *I learned as never before that persistent calling upon the Lord breaks through every stronghold of the devil, for nothing is impossible with God. For Christians in these troubled times, there is simply no other way.*

Jim Cymbala

&⁊ *The more you pray, the more you want to pray.*

John Vianney

GOD'S PERSPECTIVE

He will teach us His ways,
and we shall walk in His paths.

Isaiah 2:3 NKJV

❧ For most of us, life is busy and complicated. Amid the rush and crush of the daily grind, it is easy to lose perspective . . . easy, but wrong. When our world seems to be spinning out of control, we must seek to regain perspective by slowing ourselves down and then turning our thoughts and prayers toward God.

The familiar words of Psalm 46:10 remind us to "Be still, and know that I am God" (NKJV). When we do so, we encounter the awesome presence of our loving Heavenly Father, and we are blessed beyond words. But, when we ignore the presence of our Creator, we rob ourselves of His perspective, His peace, and His joy. Today and every day, set aside a time to be still before God. When you do, you can face the day's complications with the wisdom and power that only He can provide.

❧ *When considering the size of your problems, there are two categories that you should never worry about: the problems that are small enough for you to handle, and the ones that aren't too big for God to handle.*

Marie T. Freeman

HUMILITY IN THE PRESENCE OF THE SAVIOR

We love Him because He first loved us.

1 John 4:19 NKJV

❧ As we consider Christ's sacrifice on the cross, we should be profoundly humbled. And today, as we come to Christ in prayer, we should do so in a spirit of humble devotion.

Christ humbled Himself on a cross—for you. He shed His blood—for you. He has offered to walk with you through this life *and* throughout all eternity. As you approach Him today in prayer, think about His sacrifice and His grace. And be humble.

❧ *Do you wish to be great? Then begin by being humble. Do you desire to construct a vast and lofty fabric? Think first about the foundations of humility. The higher your structure is to be, the deeper must be its foundation.*

St. Augustine of Hippo

❧ *Let the love of Christ be believed in and felt in your hearts, and it will humble you.*

C. H. Spurgeon

❧ *Love always involves responsibility, and love always involves sacrifice. And we do not really love Christ unless we are prepared to face His task and to take up His Cross.*

William Barclay

GOD'S STRENGTH
FOR THE DAY AHEAD

And he said: "The Lord is my rock
and my fortress and my deliverer;
the God of my strength, in whom I will trust."

3 Samuel 22:2, 3 NKJV

❧ God is a never-ending source of support and courage for those of us who call upon Him. When we are weary, He gives us strength. When we see no hope, God reminds us of His promises. When we grieve, God wipes away our tears.

Do the demands of this day threaten to overwhelm you? If so, you must rely not only upon your own resources, but also upon the promises of your Father in heaven. God will hold your hand and walk with you every day of your life *if* you let Him. So even if your circumstances are difficult, trust the Father. His love is eternal and His goodness endures forever.

❧ *If we take God's program, we can have God's power—not otherwise.*

E. Stanley Jones

❧ *Let your faith in Christ be in the quiet confidence that He will, every day and every moment, keep you as the apple of His eye, keep you in perfect peace and in the sure experience of all the light and the strength you need.*

Andrew Murray

Mon

WALKING THE CHRISTIAN PATH

But as God has distributed to each one, as the Lord
has called each one, so let him walk.

1 Corinthians 7:17 NKJV

≈ Each day, as we awaken from sleep, we are confronted with countless opportunities to serve God and to follow in the footsteps of His Son. When we do, our Heavenly Father guides our steps and blesses our endeavors.

As citizens of a fast-changing world, we face challenges that sometimes leave us feeling overworked, over-committed, and overwhelmed. But God has different plans for us. He intends that we slow down long enough to praise Him and to glorify His Son. When we do, He lifts our spirits and enriches our lives.

Today provides a glorious opportunity to place yourself in the service of the One who is the Giver of all blessings. May you seek His will, may you trust His word, and may you walk in the footsteps of His Son.

≈ *The Bible says that being a Christian is not only a great way to die, but it's also the best way to live.*

Bill Hybels

≈ *When we invite Jesus into our lives, we experience life in the fullest, most vital sense.*

Catherine Marshall

PRAISE FOR THE FATHER; THANKS FOR HIS BLESSINGS

I will praise You with my whole heart.

Psalm 138:1 NKJV

&. The words by Fanny Crosby are familiar: "This is my story, this is my song, praising my Savior, all the day long." As believers who have been saved by the blood of a risen Christ, we must do exactly as the song instructs: We must praise our Savior time and time again throughout the day. Worship and praise should be a part of everything we do. Otherwise, we quickly lose perspective as we fall prey to the demands of everyday life.

Do you sincerely desire to be a worthy servant of the One who has given you eternal love and eternal life? Then praise Him for who He is and for what He has done for you. And don't just praise Him on Sunday morning. Praise Him all day long, every day, for as long as you live . . . and then for all eternity.

&. *The time for universal praise is sure to come some day. Let us begin to do our part now.*

Hannah Whitall Smith

&. *I am to praise God for all things, regardless of where they seem to originate. Doing this is the key to receiving the blessings of God. Praise will wash away my resentments.*

Catherine Marshall

PRAYING TO KNOW GOD

Teach me Your way, O Lord;
I will walk in Your truth.

Psalm 86:11 NKJV

&o Andrew Murray observed, "Some people pray just to pray, and some people pray to know God." Your task, as maturing believer, is to pray, not out of habit or obligation, but out of a sincere desire to know your Heavenly Father. Through constant prayers, you should petition God, you should praise Him, and you seek to discover His unfolding plans for your life.

Today, reach out to the Giver of all blessings. Turn to Him for guidance and for strength. Invite Him into every corner of your day. Ask Him to teach you *and* to lead you. And remember that no matter what your circumstances, God is never far away; He is here . . . always right here. So pray.

&o *The purpose of all prayer is to find God's will and to make that will our prayer.*

Catherine Marshall

&o *There is a communion with God that asks for nothing, yet asks for everything . . . . He who seeks the Father more than anything he can give is likely to have what he asks, for he is not likely to ask amiss.*

George MacDonald

THE COURAGE TO RISK FAILURE

The fear of man brings a snare,
but whoever trusts in the Lord shall be safe.

Proverbs 29:25 NKJV

❧ As we consider the uncertainties of the future, we are confronted with a powerful temptation: The temptation to "play it safe." Unwilling to move mountains, we fret over molehills. Unwilling to entertain great hopes for the tomorrow, we focus on the unfairness of the today. Unwilling to trust God completely, we take timid half-steps when God intends that we make giant leaps.

Today, ask God for the courage to step beyond the boundaries of your doubts. Ask Him to guide you to a place where you can realize your full potential—a place where you are freed from the fear of failure. Ask Him to do *His* part, and promise Him that you will do *your* part. Don't ask Him to lead you to a "safe" place; ask Him to lead you to the "right" place . . . and remember: Those two places are seldom the same.

❧ *Do not be one of those who, rather than risk failure, never attempt anything.*

Thomas Merton

❧ *How beautiful it is to learn that grace isn't fragile, and that in the family of God we can fail and not be a failure.*

Gloria Gaither

WHEN HIS PEACE BECOMES OUR PEACE

But now in Christ Jesus you who once were far off
have been brought near by the blood of Christ.
For He Himself is our peace.

Ephesians 2:13, 14 NKJV

   Have you found the genuine peace that can be yours through Jesus Christ? Or are you still rushing after the illusion of "peace and happiness" that the world promises but cannot deliver?

The beautiful words of John 14:27 remind us that Jesus offers us peace, not as the world gives, but as He alone gives: "Peace I leave with you, My peace I give to you; not as the world gives do I give to you. Let not your heart be troubled, neither let it be afraid" (NKJV). Our challenge is to accept Christ's peace and then, as best we can, to share His blessings with our neighbors.

Today, as a gift to yourself, to your family, and to the world, let Christ's peace become your peace. Let Him rule your heart and your thoughts. When you do, you will partake in the peace that only He can give.

   The life of strain is difficult. The life of inner peace—a life that comes from a positive attitude—is the easiest type of existence.

Norman Vincent Peale

SEARCHING FOR THE RIGHT KIND OF TREASURE

For where your treasure is,
there your heart will be also.

Luke 12:34 NKJV

   All of mankind is engaged in a colossal, worldwide treasure hunt. Some people seek treasure from earthly sources, treasures such as material wealth or public acclaim; others seek God's treasures by making Him the cornerstone of their lives.

What kind of treasure hunter are you? Are you so caught up in the demands of everyday living that you sometimes allow the search for worldly treasures to become your primary focus? If so, it's time to reorganize your daily to-do list by placing God in His rightful place: first place. Don't allow anyone or anything to separate you from your Heavenly Father and His only begotten Son.

The world's treasures are difficult to find and difficult to keep; God's treasures are ever-present and everlasting. Which treasures, then, will you claim as your own?

   Anything that makes religion a second object makes it no object. He who offers to God a second place offers him no place.

John Ruskin

HONOR FOR THE RIGHTEOUS

He who follows righteousness and mercy finds life,
righteousness and honor.

Proverbs 21:21 NKJV

❧ If you wish to be honored by your peers, you must lead a life that *appears* to be honorable. But, if you seek honor from God, you must not only behave honorably, you must also be motivated by *righteous intentions*. Why? Because God knows your heart.

Who will you try to please today: God or man? Your obligation is most certainly *not* to imperfect men or women. Your obligation is to an all-knowing and perfect God. Trust Him always. Love Him always. Praise Him always. Seek to please Him and *only* Him. Always. And then, receive the only honor that really counts: His.

❧ *The soul of a righteous person is nothing but a paradise, in which, as God tells us, he takes his delight.*

Teresa of Avila

❧ *We must appropriate the tender mercy of God every day after conversion, or problems quickly develop. We need his grace daily in order to live a righteous life.*

Jim Cymbala

STEERING CLEAR OF THE ROAD TO RUIN

Innocent people will be kept safe, but those who are dishonest will suddenly be ruined.

Proverbs 28:18 NCV

❧ How hard is it to bump into temptation in this crazy world? Not very hard. The devil, it seems, is causing pain and heartache in more places and in more ways than ever before. We, as Christians, must remain vigilant. Not only must we resist Satan when he confronts us, but we must also avoid those places where Satan can most easily tempt us. And, if we are to avoid the unending temptations of this world, we must earnestly wrap ourselves in the protection of God's Holy Word.

The road to ruin is wide, long, and deadly. Avoid it, and help others do the same. When you do, God will smile—and the devil won't.

❧ *The redemption, accomplished for us by our Lord Jesus Christ on the cross at Calvary, is redemption from the power of sin as well as from its guilt. Christ is able to save all who come unto God by Him.*

Hannah Whitall Smith

❧ *Good and evil both increase at compound interest. That is why the little decisions you and I make every day are of such infinite importance.*

C. S. Lewis

FROM THE INSIDE OUT

For indeed, the kingdom of God is within you.
Luke 17:21 NKJV

&o If we sincerely want to change ourselves for the better, we must start on the inside and work our way out from there. Lasting change doesn't occur "out there"; it occurs "in here." It occurs, not in the shifting sands of our own particular circumstances, but in quiet depths of our own hearts.

Do you desire to improve some aspect of your life? If so, don't expect changing circumstances to miraculously transform you into the person you want to become. Transformation starts with God, and it starts in the silent center of a humble human heart—like yours.

&o *We're prone to want God to change our circumstances, but He wants to change our character. We think that peace comes from the outside in, but it comes from the inside out.*

Warren Wiersbe

&o *For God is, indeed, a wonderful Father who longs to pour out His mercy upon us, and whose majesty is so great that He can transform us from deep within.*

Teresa of Avila

LEARNING FROM THE FAITHFUL

*We have around us many people whose lives tell us
what faith means. So let us run the race that is before
us and never give up. We should remove from
our lives anything that would get in the way
and the sin that so easily holds us back.*

Hebrews 12:1 NCV

❧ It has been said on many occasions that life is
a team sport. So, too, is learning how to live. If
we are to become mature believers—and if seek to
discover God's purposes in our everyday lives—we
need worthy examples and wise mentors.
Are you walking with the wise? Are you spending
time with people you admire? Are you learning
how to live from people who know how to live? If
you genuinely seek to walk with God, then you will
walk with those who walk with Him.

❧ *We urgently need people who encourage and inspire
us to move toward God and away from the world's
enticing pleasures.*

Jim Cymbala

❧ *Let us preach you, Dear Jesus, without preaching,
not by words but by our example, by the casting force,
the sympathetic influence of what we do, the evident
fullness of the love our hearts bear to you. Amen.*

Mother Teresa

this

FACING OUR RESPONSIBILITIES

*We want each of you to go on with the same hard
work all your lives so you will surely get what
you hope for. We do not want you to become lazy.
Be like those who through faith and patience
will receive what God has promised.*

Hebrews 6:11, 12 NCV

&o These words from the sixth chapter of Hebrews remind us that as Christians we must labor diligently, patiently, and faithfully. Do you want to be a worthy example for your family and friends? If so, you must preach the gospel of responsible behavior, not only with your words, but also by your actions.

&o *If you seek to know the path of your duty, use God as your compass.*

C. H. Spurgeon

&o *Every time you refuse to face up to life and its problems, you weaken your character.*

E. Stanley Jones

&o *Jesus knows one of the greatest barriers to our faith is often our unwillingness to be made whole— our unwillingness to accept responsibility—our unwillingness to live without excuse for our spiritual smallness and immaturity.*

Anne Graham Lotz

SERVING GOD . . . WITH HUMILITY

Jesus sat down and called the twelve apostles to him.
He said, "Whoever wants to be the most important
must be last of all and servant of all."

Mark 9:35 NCV

&co; The teachings of Jesus are clear: We achieve greatness through service to others. Jesus teaches us that the most esteemed men and women are not the self-congratulatory leaders of society but are instead the humblest of servants.

Today, you may feel the temptation to build yourself up in the eyes of your neighbors. Resist that temptation. Instead, serve your neighbors quietly and without fanfare. Find a need and fill it…humbly. Lend a helping hand and share a word of kindness…anonymously, for this is God's way.

As a humble servant, you will glorify yourself not before men, but before God, and that's what God intends. After all, earthly glory is fleeting, but heavenly glory endures throughout eternity. So, the choice is yours: Either you can lift yourself up here on earth and be humbled in heaven, or vice versa. Choose vice versa.

&co; *Because Christ Jesus came to the world clothed in humility, he will always be found among those who are clothed with humility. He will be found among the humble people.*

A. W. Tozer

DISCERNING SPIRITUAL TRUTHS

_A person who does not have the Spirit does not
accept the truths that come from the Spirit of God.
That person thinks they are foolish and cannot
understand them, because they can only be judged to
be true by the Spirit. The spiritual person is able to
judge all things, but no one can judge him._

1 Corinthians 2:14, 15 NCV

❧ When God's spirit touches our hearts, we are
confronted by a powerful force: the awesome,
irresistible force of God's Truth. In response to that
force, we will either follow God's lead by allowing
Him to guide our thoughts and deeds, or we will
resist God's calling and accept the consequences of
our rebellion.

Today, as you fulfill the responsibilities that God
has placed before you, ask yourself this question:
"Do my thoughts and actions bear witness to the
ultimate Truth that God has placed in my heart,
or am I allowing the pressures of everyday life to
overwhelm me?" It's a profound question that only
you can answer. You be the judge.

❧ _Learning God's truth and getting it into our heads is
one thing, but living God's truth and getting it into our
characters is quite something else._

Warren Wiersbe

Happy Tomorrow

Whereas you do not know what will happen tomorrow. For what is your life? It is even a vapor that appears for a little time and then vanishes away.

James 4:14 NJKV

❧ When will you rejoice at God's marvelous creation? Today or tomorrow? When will you accept His abundance: now or later? When will you accept the peace that can *and should* be yours? In the present moment or in the distant future? The answer, of course, is straightforward: The best moment to accept God's gifts is the present one.

Will you accept God's blessings now or later? Are you willing to give Him your full attention today? Hopefully so. He deserves it. And so, for that matter, do you.

❧ *Men spend their lives in anticipation, in determining to be vastly happy at some period or other, when they have time. But the present time has one advantage over every other: it is ours.*

Charles Caleb Colton

❧ *God gave you this glorious day. Don't disappoint Him. Use it for His glory.*

Marie T. Freeman

❧ *Let's quit singing "Sweet By-and-by" and start singing "Sweet Now-and-now."*

Sam Jones

Mon

BUSY WITH OUR THOUGHTS

*So prepare your minds for service
and have self-control.*

1 Peter 1:13 NCV

Because we are human, we are always busy with our thoughts. We simply can't help ourselves. Our brains never shut off, and even while we're sleeping, we mull things over in our minds. The question is not *if* we will think; the question is *how* will we think and *what* will we think about.

Today, focus your thoughts on God and His will. And if you've been plagued by pessimism and doubt, stop thinking like that! Place your faith in God and give thanks for His blessings. Think optimistically about your world and your life. It's the wise way to use your mind. And besides, since you will always be busy with your thoughts, you might as well make those thoughts pleasing (to God) and helpful (to you and yours).

Occupy your minds with good thoughts, or the enemy will fill them with bad ones. Unoccupied, they cannot be.

Thomas More

Feelings of confidence depend upon the type of thoughts you habitually occupy. Think defeat, and you are bound to be defeated.

Norman Vincent Peale

COMPASSION AND COURTESY IN A DISCOURTEOUS WORLD

*Finally, all of you be of one mind,
having compassion for one another; love as brothers,
be tenderhearted, be courteous.*

1 Peter 3:8 NKJV

🐚 As Christians, we are instructed to be courteous and compassionate. As believers, we are called to be gracious, humble, gentle, and kind. But sometimes, we fall short. Sometimes, amid the busyness and confusion of everyday life, we may neglect to share a kind word or a kind deed. This oversight hurts others, and it hurts us as well.

Today, slow yourself down and be alert for those who need your smile, your kind words, or your helping hand. Make kindness a centerpiece of your dealings with others. They will be blessed, and you will be, too. So make this promise to yourself and keep it: Honor Christ by obeying His Golden Rule. He deserves no less. And neither, for that matter, do they.

🐚 *He who sows courtesy reaps friendship, and he who plants kindness gathers love.*

Basil the Great

🐚 *While great brilliance and intellect are to be admired, they cannot dry one tear or mend a broken spirit. Only kindness can accomplish this.*

John Drescher

Wed

WHOM WE SHOULD JUDGE

Judge not, and you shall not be judged.
Condemn not, and you shall not be condemned.
Forgive, and you will be forgiven.

Luke 6:37 NKJV

  Even the most devoted Christians may fall prey to a powerful yet subtle temptation: the temptation to judge others. But as faithful believers, we are commanded to refrain from such behavior. The warning of Luke 6:37 is clear: "Judge not."

We are warned that to judge others is to invite fearful consequences: To the extent we judge *them*, so, too, will *we* be judged by God. Let us refrain, then, from judging our neighbors. Instead, let us forgive them and love them in the same way that God has forgiven us.

  Turn your attention upon yourself and beware of judging the deeds of other men, for in judging others a man labors vainly, often makes mistakes, and easily sins; whereas, in judging and taking stock of himself he does something that is always profitable.

Thomas à Kempis

  Christians think they are prosecuting attorneys or judges, when, in reality, God has called all of us to be witnesses.

Warren Wiersbe

WISDOM FROM THE HEART

But the fruit of the Spirit is love, joy, peace, longsuffering, kindness, goodness, faithfulness, gentleness, self-control. Against such there is no law.

Galatians 5:22, 23 NKJV

❧ When we genuinely open our hearts to God, He speaks to us through a small, still voice within. When He does, we can listen, or not. When we pay careful attention to the Father, He leads us along a path of His choosing, a path that leads to abundance, peace, joy, and eternal life. But when we choose to ignore God, we select a path that is not His, and we must endure the consequences of our shortsightedness.

Today, focus your thoughts and your prayers on the path that God intends for you to take. When you do, your loving Heavenly Father will speak to your heart. When He does, listen carefully . . . and trust Him.

❧ *Christ teaches by the Spirit of wisdom in the heart, opening the understanding to the Spirit of revelation in the word.*

Matthew Henry

❧ *Wisdom is knowledge applied. Head knowledge is useless on the battlefield. Knowledge stamped on the heart makes one wise.*

Beth Moore

THINK NOW, ACT LATER

Enthusiasm without knowledge is not good.
If you act too quickly, you might make a mistake.

Proverbs 19:2 NCV

➿ God's Word is clear: As believers, we are called to lead lives of discipline, diligence, moderation, and maturity. But the world often tempts us to behave otherwise. Everywhere we turn, or so it seems, we are faced with powerful temptations to behave in undisciplined, ungodly ways.

God's Word instructs us to be disciplined in our thoughts *and* our actions; God's Word warns us against the dangers of impulsive behavior. As believers in a just God, we should think *and* react accordingly.

➿ *Zeal without knowledge is always less useful and effective than regulated zeal, and very often is highly dangerous.*

Bernard of Clairvaux

➿ *We will always experience regret when we live for the moment and do not weigh our words and deeds before we give them life.*

Lisa Bevere

THE GIFT OF GRACE

For by grace you have been saved through faith,
and that not of yourselves; it is the gift of God.

Ephesians 2:8 NKJV

❧ God has given us so many gifts, but none can compare with the gift of salvation. We have not earned our salvation; it is a gift from God. When we accept Christ into our hearts, we are saved by His grace.

The familiar words of Ephesians 2:8 make God's promise perfectly clear: It is by grace we have been saved, through faith. We are saved not because of our good deeds but because of our faith in Christ.

God's grace is the ultimate gift, and we owe to Him the ultimate in thanksgiving. Let us praise the Creator for this priceless blessing, and let us share the Good News with all who cross our paths. We return our Father's love by accepting His grace and by sharing His message and His love. When we do, we are eternally blessed . . . and the Father smiles.

❧ *The man who lives without Jesus is the poorest of the poor, whereas no one is so rich as the man who lives in His grace.*

Thomas à Kempis

❧ *The life of faith is a daily exploration of the constant and countless ways in which God's grace and love are experienced.*

Eugene Peterson

PROBLEM-SOLVING 101

*People who do what is right may have many problems,
but the Lord will solve them all.*

Psalm 34:19 NCV

  Life is an exercise in problem-solving. The question is not *whether* we will encounter problems; the real question is how we will choose to address them. When it comes to solving the problems of everyday living, we often know precisely what needs to be done, but we may be slow in doing it—especially if what needs to be done is difficult or uncomfortable for us. So we put off till tomorrow what should be done today.

  The words of Psalm 34 remind us that the Lord solves problems for "people who do what is right." And usually, doing "what is right" means doing the uncomfortable work of confronting our problems sooner rather than later. So with no further ado, let the problem-solving begin . . . now.

  Faith does not eliminate problems. Faith keeps you in a trusting relationship with God in the midst of your problems.

Henry Blackaby

  Always remember that problems contain values that have improvement potential.

Norman Vincent Peale

Your Shining Light

You are the light of the world. A city that is set on a hill cannot be hidden. Nor do they light a lamp and put it under a basket, but on a lampstand, and it gives light to all who are in the house. Let your light so shine before men, that they may see your good works and glorify your Father in heaven.

Matthew 5:14–16 NKJV

❧ Whether we like it or not, we are role models. Hopefully, the lives we lead and the choices we make will serve as enduring examples of the spiritual abundance that is available to all who worship God and obey His commandments.

Ask yourself this question: Are you the kind of role model that *you* would want to emulate? If so, congratulations. But if certain aspects of your behavior could stand improvement, the best day to begin your self-improvement regimen is this one. Because whether you realize it or not, people you love are watching your behavior, and they're learning how to live. You owe to them—and to yourself—to live righteously and well.

❧ *If you want your neighbor to know what Christ will do for him, let the neighbor see what Christ has done for you.*

Henry Ward Beecher

GOD'S PERFECT LOVE

*This is what real love is: It is not our love for God;
it is God's love for us in sending his Son
to be the way to take away our sins.*

1 John 4:10 NCV

&o God is love, and God's love is perfect. When we open our hearts to His perfect love, we are touched by the Creator's hand, and we are transformed, not just for a day, but for all eternity.

Today, as you carve out quiet moments of thanksgiving and praise for your Creator, open yourself to His presence and to His love.

&o *God proved his love on the cross. When Christ hung, and bled, and died it was God saying to the world—I love you.*

Billy Graham

&o *Jesus loves us with fidelity, purity, constancy, and passion, no matter how imperfect we are.*

Stormie Omartian

&o *There is no creature made who can realize how much, how sweetly, and how tenderly our Maker loves us. And therefore we can, with His grace and His help, stand in spirit, gazing with endless wonder at this lofty, immeasurable love—beyond human scope—that the Almighty, in His goodness, has for us.*

Juliana of Norwich

SUCCESS ACCORDING TO GOD

*Live the way the Lord your God has commanded you
so that you may live and have what is good.*

Deuteronomy 5:33 NCV

&o How do you define success? Do you define it as the accumulation of material possessions or the adulation of your neighbors? If so, you need to reorder your priorities. Genuine success has little to do with fame or fortune; it has everything to do with God's gift of love and with His promise of salvation.

If you have allowed Christ to reign over your life, you are already a towering success in the eyes of God, but there is still more that you can do. You task—as a believer who has been touched by the Creator's grace—is to accept the spiritual abundance and peace that He offers through the person of His Son. Then, you can share the healing message of God's love and His abundance with a world that desperately needs both. When you do, you have reached the pinnacle of success.

&o *God didn't call us to be successful, just faithful.*

Mother Teresa

&o *People judge us by the success of our efforts. God looks at the efforts themselves.*

Charlotte Brontë

FEARS IN PERSPECTIVE

They won't be afraid of bad news;
their hearts are steady because they trust the Lord.

Psalm 112:7 NCV

❧ Most of the things we worry about will never come to pass, yet we worry still. We worry about the future and the past; we worry about finances and relationships. As we survey the landscape of our lives, we observe all manner of molehills and imagine them to be mountains.

Are you concerned about the inevitable challenges that make up the fabric of everyday life? If so, why not ask God to help you regain a clear perspective about the problems (and opportunities) that confront you? When you petition Your Heavenly Father sincerely and seek His guidance, He can touch your heart, clear your vision, renew your mind, and calm your fears.

❧ *Do not build up obstacles in your imagination. Difficulties must be studied and dealt with, but they must not be magnified by fear.*

Norman Vincent Peale

❧ *Earthly fears are no fears at all. Answer the big question of eternity, and the little questions of life fall into perspective.*

Max Lucado

THE MIGHTY WORKS OF THOSE WHO BELIEVE

Most assuredly, I say to you, he who believes in Me,
the works that I do he will do also.

John 14:12 NKJV

  When you invite Christ to rule over your heart, you avail yourself of His power. And make no mistake about it: You and Christ, working together, can do miraculous things. In fact, miraculous things are _exactly_ what Christ intends for you to do, but He won't _force you_ to do great things on His behalf. The decision to become a full-fledged participant in His power is a decision that you must make for yourself.

  The words of John 14:12 make this promise: When you put absolute faith in Christ, you can share in His power. Today, trust the Savior's promise and expect a miracle in His name.

  We must understand that the first and chief thing—for everyone who would do the work of Jesus—is to believe, and in doing so, to become linked to Him, the Almighty One...and then, to pray the prayer of faith in His Name.

Andrew Murray

  In the fulfillment of your duties, let your intentions be so pure that you reject from your actions any other motive than the glory of God and the salvation of souls.

Angela Merici

GUARDING OUR THOUGHTS

Those who are pure in their thinking are happy,
because they will be with God.

Matthew 5:8 NCV

Paul Valéry observed, "We hope vaguely but dread precisely." All too often, we allow the worries of everyday life to overwhelm our thoughts and cloud our vision. What is needed is clearer perspective, renewed faith, and a different focus.

When we focus on the frustrations of today or the uncertainties of tomorrow, we rob ourselves of peace in the present moment. But, when we focus on God's grace, and when we trust in the ultimate wisdom of God's plan for our lives, our worries no longer tyrannize us.

Today, remember that God is infinitely greater than the challenges that you face. Remember also that your thoughts are profoundly powerful, so guard them accordingly.

Our own possible bad thoughts and deeds are far more dangerous to us than any enemy from the world.

Ambrose of Milan

No more imperfect thoughts. No more sad memories. No more ignorance. My redeemed body will have a redeemed mind. Grant me a foretaste of that perfect mind as you mirror your thoughts in me today.

Joni Eareckson Tada

GOD HAS A REASON

For this reason we also, since the day we heard it,
do not cease to pray for you, and to ask that
you may be filled with the knowledge of His will
in all wisdom and spiritual understanding

Colossians 1:9 NKJV

⁋ As the journey through this life unfolds day by day, we are confronted with situations that we simply don't understand. But God does. And He has a reason for everything that He does. Furthermore, God doesn't explain Himself in ways that we, as mortals with limited insight and clouded vision, can comprehend. So, instead of understanding every aspect of God's unfolding plan for our lives and our universe, we must be satisfied to trust Him completely. We cannot know God's motivations, nor can we understand His actions. We can, however, trust Him, and we must.

⁋ *God is God. He knows what he is doing. When you can't trace his hand, trust his heart.*

Max Lucado

⁋ *Every decision God makes is a good and right decision, so we can be certain that every decision God makes regarding us will be a right one.*

Bill Hybels

Mon

FAITH ABOVE FEELINGS

Now the just shall live by faith.

Hebrews 10:38 NKJV

  Hebrews 10:38 teaches that we should live by faith. Yet sometimes, despite our best intentions, negative feelings can rob us of the peace and abundance that would otherwise be ours through Christ. When anger or anxiety separates us from the spiritual blessings that God has in store, we must rethink our priorities and renew our faith. And we must place faith above feelings.

Human emotions are highly variable, decidedly unpredictable, and often unreliable. Our emotions are like the weather, only far more fickle. So we must learn to live by faith, not by the ups and downs of our own emotional roller coasters.

Sometime during this day, you will probably be gripped by a strong negative emotion. Distrust it. Reign it in. Test it. And turn it over to God. Your emotions will inevitably change; God will not. So trust Him completely as you watch your feelings slowly evaporate into thin air—which, of course, they will.

  The spiritual life is a life beyond moods. It is a life in which we choose joy and do not allow ourselves to become victims of passing feelings of happiness or depression.

Henri Nouwen

BEYOND ENVY

*Let us walk properly, as in the day, not in revelry
and drunkenness, not in lewdness and lust,
not in strife and envy.*

Romans 13:13 NKJV

Because we are frail, imperfect human beings, we are sometimes envious of others. But God's Word warns us that envy is sin. Thus, we must guard ourselves against the natural tendency to feel resentment and jealousy when other people experience good fortune.

As believers, we have absolutely no reason to be envious of any people on earth. After all, as Christians we are already recipients of the greatest gift in all creation: God's grace. We have been promised the gift of eternal life through God's only begotten Son, and we must count that gift as our most precious possession.

Rather than succumbing to the sin of envy, we should focus on the marvelous things that God has done for us—starting with Christ's sacrifice. And we must refrain from preoccupying ourselves with the blessings that God has chosen to give others. So here's a surefire formula for a happier, healthier life: Count your own blessings and let your neighbors counts theirs. It's the godly way to live.

How can you possess the miseries of envy when you possess in Christ the best of all portions?

C. H. Spurgeon

Wed

GOD FIRST

But seek first the kingdom of God
and His righteousness, and all these things
shall be added to you.

Matthew 6:33 NKJV

❧ As you organize your day and your life, where does God fit in? Do you "squeeze Him in" on Sundays and at mealtimes? Or do you consult Him on a moment-to-moment basis? The answer to this question will determine the direction of your life's journey, the quality of that journey, and its ultimate destination.

As you consider your plans for the day ahead, organize your life around this simple principle: "God first." When you place your Creator where He belongs—at the very center of your day *and* your life—the rest of your priorities will fall into place.

❧ *Jesus Christ is the first and last, author and finisher, beginning and end, alpha and omega, and by Him all other things hold together. He must be first or nothing. God never comes next!*

Vance Havner

❧ *Oh, that we might discern the will of God, surrender to His calling, resign the masses of activities, and do a few things well. What a legacy that would be for our children.*

Beth Moore

ENTHUSIASM FOR LIFE AND FOR WORK

Do your work with enthusiasm.
Work as if you were serving the Lord,
not as if you were serving only men and women.

Ephesians 6:7 NCV

⁋ Do you see each day as a glorious opportunity to serve God and to do His will? Are you enthused about life, or do you struggle through each day giving scarcely a thought to God's blessings? Are you constantly praising God for His gifts, and are you sharing His Good News with the world? And are you excited about the possibilities for service that God has placed before you, whether at home, at work, at church, or at school? You should be.

You are the recipient of Christ's sacrificial love. Accept it with enthusiastically and share it fervently. Jesus deserves your enthusiasm; the world deserves it; and *you* deserve the experience of sharing it.

⁋ *Those who are fired with an enthusiastic idea and who allow it to take hold and dominate their thoughts find that new worlds open for them. As long as enthusiasm holds out, so will new opportunities.*

Norman Vincent Peale

HELPING TO BEAR THE BURDENS

Bear one another's burdens,
and so fulfill the law of Christ.

Galatians 6:2 NKJV

&o Neighbors. We know that we are instructed to love them, and yet there's so little time…and we're so busy. No matter. As Christians, we are commanded by our Lord and Savior Jesus Christ to love our neighbors just as we love ourselves. We are not *asked* to love our neighbors, nor are we *encouraged* to do so. We are *commanded* to love them. Period.

This very day, you will encounter someone who needs a word of encouragement, or a pat on the back, or a helping hand, or a heartfelt prayer. And, if you don't reach out to that person, who will? If you don't take the time to understand the needs of your neighbors, who will? If you don't love your brothers and sisters, who will? So, today, look for a neighbor in need…and then do something to help. Father's orders.

&o *He climbs highest who helps another up.*

Zig Ziglar

&o *What is your focus today? Joy comes when it is Jesus first, others second…then you.*

Kay Arthur

ENTRUSTING OUR HOPES TO GOD

*You, Lord, give true peace to those
who depend on you, because they trust you.*

Isaiah 26:3 NCV

❧ Have you ever felt hope for the future slipping away? If so, you have temporarily lost sight of the hope that we, as believers, must place in the promises of our Heavenly Father. If you are feeling discouraged, worried, or worse, remember the words of Psalm 31:24: "Be of good courage, and He shall strengthen your heart, all you who hope in the Lord" (NKJV).

Of course, we will face disappointments and failures, but these are only temporary defeats. Of course, this world can be a place of trials and tribulations, but we are secure. God has promised us peace, joy, and eternal life. And God keeps His promises today, tomorrow, and forever.

❧ *It is more serious to lose hope than to sin*

John of Carpathos

❧ *Christ has turned all our sunsets into dawn.*

Clement of Alexandria

THE FRUITS OF OUR LABORS

Now he who plants and he who waters are one,
and each one will receive his own reward
according to his own labor.

1 Corinthians 3:8 NKJV

&. It has been said that there are no shortcuts to any place worth going. And for believers, it's important to remember that hard work is not simply a proven way to get ahead, it's also part of God's plan for His children.

Of this we can be sure: God did not create us for lives of mediocrity; He created us for far greater things. Earning great things usually requires work and lots of it, which is perfectly fine with God. After all, He knows that we're up to the task, and He has big plans for us. Very big plans....

&. *Thank God every morning when you get up that you have something which must be done, whether you like it or not. Work breeds a hundred virtues that idleness never knows.*

Charles Kingsley

&. *Every tub must stand on its own bottom.*

Thomas Fuller

&. *Ordinary work, which is what most of us do most of the time, is ordained by God every bit as much as is the extraordinary.*

Elisabeth Elliot

PREPARING FOR THE DAY AHEAD

*So prepare your minds for service and have
self-control. All your hope should be for
the gift of grace that will be yours when
Jesus Christ is shown to you.*

1 Peter 1:13 NCV

How do you prepare for the day ahead? Do you awaken early enough to spend at least a few moments with God? Or do you sleep until the last possible minute, leaving no time to invest in matters of the heart and soul? Hopefully, you make a habit of spending precious moments each morning with your Creator. When you do, He will fill your heart, He will direct your thoughts, and He will guide your steps.

Your daily devotional time can be habit-forming, and should be. The first few minutes of each day are invaluable. Treat them that way, and offer them to God.

The mind is like a clock that is constantly running down. It has to be wound up daily with good thoughts.

Fulton J. Sheen

If I should neglect prayer but a single day, I should lose a great deal of the fire of faith.

Martin Luther

A Faith Bigger Than Fear

*Let not your heart be troubled;
you believe in God, believe also in Me.*

John 14:1 NKJV

❧ American clergyman Edward Everett Hale observed, "Some people bear three kinds of trouble—the ones they've had, the ones they have, and the ones they expect to have." How true. But a better strategy for you is this: Accept the past, live in the present, and place the future in God's capable hands.

As you face the challenges of everyday life, you may be comforted by this fact: Trouble, of every kind, is temporary. Yet God's grace is eternal. And worries, of every kind, are temporary. But God's love is everlasting. The troubles that concern you will pass. God remains. And with these thoughts in mind, it's now time for you to place *today's* troubles in their proper perspective.

❧ *Worry and anxiety are sand in the machinery of life; faith is the oil.*

E. Stanley Jones

❧ *It is not work that's kills, but worry. And, it is amazing how much wear and tear the human mind and spirit can stand if it is free from friction and well-oiled by the Spirit.*

Vance Havner

FINDING FULFILLMENT
IN ALL THE RIGHT PLACES

I am the door. If anyone enters by Me,
he will be saved.

John 10:9 NKJV

&o Where can we find contentment? Is it a result of wealth, or power, or beauty, or fame? Hardly. Genuine contentment is a gift from God to those who trust Him and follow His commandments.

Our modern world seems preoccupied with the search for happiness. We are bombarded with messages telling us that happiness depends upon the acquisition of material possessions. These messages are false. Enduring peace is not the result of our acquisitions; it is a spiritual gift from God to those who obey Him and accept His will.

If we don't find contentment in God, we will never find it anywhere else. But, if we seek Him and obey Him, we will be blessed with an inner peace that is beyond human understanding. When God dwells at the center of our lives, peace and contentment will belong to us just as surely as we belong to God.

&o *We will never be happy until we make God the source of our fulfillment and the answer to our longings.*

Stormie Omartian

Energy for Today

Let us run with endurance the race that is set before us, looking unto Jesus, the author and finisher of our faith, who for the joy that was set before Him endured the cross, despising the shame, and has sat down at the right hand of the throne of God.

Hebrews 12:1, 2 NKJV

    ❧ All of us have moments when we feel drained. All of us suffer through difficult days, trying times, and perplexing periods of our lives. Thankfully, God stands ready and willing to give us comfort and strength *if* we turn to Him.

    Burning the candle at both ends is tempting but potentially destructive. Instead, we should place first things first by saying no to the things that we simply don't have the time or the energy to do. And as we establish our priorities, we should turn to God and to His Holy Word for guidance.

    If you're a person with too many demands and too few hours in which to meet them, don't fret. Instead, focus upon God and upon His love for you. Then, ask Him for the wisdom to prioritize your life and the strength to fulfill your responsibilities. God will give you the energy to do the most important things on today's to-do list…if you ask Him.

    ❧ *Where there is much prayer, there will be much of the Spirit; where there is much of the Spirit, there will be ever-increasing power.*

Andrew Murray

THE COURAGE TO FOLLOW GOD

Be strong and of good courage, and do it;
do not fear nor be dismayed, for the Lord God—
my God—will be with you. He will not leave you
nor forsake you, until you have finished all
the work for the service of the house of the Lord.

1 Chronicles 28:20 NKJV

❧ Because we are saved by a risen Christ, we can have hope for the future, no matter how desperate our circumstances may seem. After all, God has promised that we are His throughout eternity. And, He has told us that we must place our hopes in Him.

Today, summon the courage to follow God. Even if the path seems difficult, even if your heart is fearful, trust your Heavenly Father and follow Him. Trust Him with your day *and* your life. Do His work, care for His children, and share His Good News. Let Him guide your steps. He will not lead you astray.

❧ *Down through the centuries, in times of trouble and trial, God has brought courage to the hearts of those who love Him. The Bible is filled with assurances of God's help and comfort in every kind of trouble which might cause fears to arise in the human heart. You can look ahead with promise, hope, and joy.*

Billy Graham

Sat

WELCOMING THE NEW YOU

*You were taught to leave your old self—to stop living
the evil way you lived before. That old self becomes
worse, because people are fooled by the evil things
they want to do. But you were taught to be made
new in your hearts, to become a new person.
That new person is made to be like God—
made to be truly good and holy.*

Ephesians 4:22–24 NCV

⚘ Think, for a moment, about the "old" you, the person you were before you invited Christ to reign over your heart. Now, think about the "new" you, the person you have become since then. Is there a difference between the "old" you and the "new and improved" version? There should be! And that difference should be noticeable not only to you but also to others.

The Bible clearly teaches that when we welcome Christ into our hearts, we become new creations through Him. Our challenge, of course, is to *behave ourselves* like new creations. When we do, God fills our hearts; He blesses our endeavors; and He transforms our lives . . . forever.

⚘ *Jesus divided people—everyone—into two classes—the once-born and the twice-born, the unconverted and the converted. No other distinction mattered.*

E. Stanley Jones

A Healthy Fear

The fear of the Lord is the beginning of wisdom;
a good understanding have all those who do
His commandments. His praise endures forever.

Psalm 111:10 NKJV

❧ The Bible instructs us that a healthy fear of the Lord is the foundation of wisdom. Yet sometimes, in our shortsightedness, we fail to show respect for our Creator because we fail to obey Him. When we do, our disobedience *always* has consequences, and *sometimes* those consequences are severe.

When we honor the Father by obeying His commandments, we receive His love and His grace. Today, let us demonstrate our respect for God by developing a *healthy* fear of disobeying Him.

❧ *It is not possible that mortal men should be thoroughly conscious of the divine presence without being filled with awe.*

C. H. Spurgeon

❧ *A healthy fear of God will do much to deter us from sin.*

Charles Swindoll

❧ *The remarkable thing about fearing God is that when you fear God, you fear nothing else, whereas if you do not fear God, you fear everything else.*

Oswald Chambers

THE ULTIMATE ARMOR

*Finally, my brethren, be strong in the Lord
and in the power of His might. Put on the whole
armor of God, that you may be able to
stand against the wiles of the devil.*

Ephesians 6:10, 11 NKJV

 ✒ In a world filled with dangers and temptations, God is the ultimate armor. In a world filled with misleading messages, God's Word is the ultimate truth. In a world filled with more frustrations than we can count, God's Son offers the ultimate peace. Will you accept God's peace and wear God's armor against the dangers of our world?

Sometimes, in the crush of everyday life, God may seem far away, but He is not. God is everywhere you have ever been and everywhere you will ever go. He is with you night and day; He knows your thoughts and your prayers. He is your ultimate Protector. And, when you earnestly seek His protection, you will find it because He is here—always—waiting patiently for you to reach out to Him.

 ✒ *In the worst temptations nothing can help us but faith that God's Son has put on flesh, sits at the right hand of the Father, and prays for us. There is no mightier comfort.*

Martin Luther

USING OUR GIFTS

I remind you to keep using the gift God gave you . . . .
Now let it grow, as a small flame grows into a fire.

2 Timothy 1:6 NCV

🌿 Every day of your life, you have a choice to make: Nurture your talents or neglect them. When you choose wisely, God rewards your efforts, and He expands your opportunities to serve Him.

We live in a world in which leisure is glorified and misbehavior is glamorized. But God has other plans. He did not create us for lives of mischief or mediocrity; He created us for far greater things. He created with the intention that we use *our* talents for *His* glory.

How will you use your God's gifts today? If you are wise, you will seek fresh opportunities to fan your own spark of talent into a roaring flame.

🌿 *Natural abilities are like natural plants; they need pruning by study.*

Francis Bacon

🌿 *There's a unique sense of fulfillment that comes when we submit our gifts to God's use and ask him to energize them in a supernatural way—and then step back to watch what he does. It can be the difference between merely existing in black and white and living a life in full, brilliant color.*

Lee Strobel

Wed

OUR PURPOSES, GOD'S PURPOSES

*For we are His workmanship, created in Christ Jesus
for good works, which God prepared beforehand
that we should walk in them.*

Ephesians 2:10 NKJV

🖎 Whenever we struggle against God's plans, we suffer. When we resist God's calling, our efforts bear little fruit. Our best strategy, therefore, is to seek God's path and to follow Him wherever He chooses to lead. When we do so, we are blessed.

When we align ourselves with God's purposes, we avail ourselves of His power and His peace. But how can we know precisely what God's intentions are? The answer, of course, is that even the most well-intentioned believers face periods of uncertainty and doubt about the direction of their lives. So, too, will you.

When you arrive at one of life's inevitable crossroads, that is precisely the moment when you should turn your thoughts and prayers toward God. When you do, He will make Himself known to you in a time and manner of His choosing.

🖎 *The born-again Christian sees life not as a blurred, confused, meaningless mass, but as something planned and purposeful.*

Billy Graham

THOUGHTFUL WORDS

The wise don't tell everything they know,
but the foolish talk too much and are ruined.

Proverbs 10:14 NCV

⚜ Think...pause...then speak: Wise is the man or woman who can communicate in this way. But all too often, in the rush to have ourselves heard, we speak first and think next...with unfortunate results.

God's Word reminds us that, "Careless words stab like a sword, but wise words bring healing" (Proverbs 12:18 NCV). If we seek to be a source of encouragement to friends and family, then we must measure our words carefully. Words are important: They can hurt or heal. Words can uplift us or discourage us, and reckless words, spoken in haste, cannot be erased.

Today, seek to encourage all who cross your path. Measure your words carefully. Speak wisely, not impulsively. Use words of kindness and praise, not words of anger or derision. Remember that you have the power to heal others or to injure them, to lift others up or to hold them back. When you lift them up, your wisdom will bring healing and comfort to a world that needs both.

⚜ *Happy the person whose words issue from the Holy Spirit and not from himself.*

Anthony of Padua

Fri

POPULARITY CONTESTS

Do you think I am trying to make people accept me?
No, God is the One I am trying to please. Am I trying
to please people? If I still wanted to please people,
I would not be a servant of Christ.

Galatians 1:10 NCV

🔖 Rick Warren observed, "Those who follow the crowd usually get lost in it." We know these words to be true, but oftentimes we fail to live by them. Instead of trusting God for guidance, we imitate our neighbors and suffer the consequences. Instead of seeking to please our Father in heaven, we strive to please our peers, with decidedly mixed results.

Whom will you try to please today: your God or your friends? Your obligation is most certainly *not* to neighbors, to friends, or even to family members. Your obligation is to an all-knowing, all-powerful God. You must seek to please Him first and always. No exceptions.

🔖 *Long ago I ceased to count heads. Truth is often in the minority in this evil world.*

C. H. Spurgeon

🔖 *What difference does it make to you what someone else becomes, or says, or does? You do not need to answer for others, only for yourself.*

Thomas à Kempis

Sat

SELF-DEFEATING ANGER

When you are angry, do not sin, and be sure to
stop being angry before the end of the day.
Do not give the devil a way to defeat you.

Ephesians 4:26, 27 NCV

When you allow yourself to become angry, you are certain to defeat at least one person: yourself. When you allow the minor frustrations of everyday life to hijack your emotions, you do harm to yourself *and* to your loved ones. So today and every day, guard yourself against the kind of angry thinking that inevitably takes a toll on your emotions *and* your relationships.

When you strike out in anger, you may miss the other person, but you will always hit yourself.

Jim Gallery

What is hatred, after all, other than anger that was allowed to remain, that has become ingrained and deep-rooted? What was anger when it was fresh becomes hatred when it is aged.

St. Augustine

Anger is a kind of temporary madness.

Basil the Great

Unrighteous anger feeds the ego and produces the poison of selfishness in the heart.

Warren Wiersbe

Sun

ACCORDING TO GOD

The counsel of the Lord stands forever,
the plans of His heart to all generations.

Psalm 33:11 NKJV

When you have a question that you simply can't answer, whom do you ask? When you face a difficult decision, to whom do you turn for counsel? To friends? To mentors? To family members? Or do you turn first to the Ultimate source of wisdom? The answers to life's Big Questions start with God and with the teachings of His Holy Word.

God's wisdom stands forever. God's Word is a light for every generation. Make it *your* light as well. Use the Bible as a compass for the next stage of your life's journey. Use it as the yardstick by which your behavior is measured. And as you carefully consult the pages of God's Word, prayerfully ask Him to reveal the wisdom that you need. When you take your concerns to God, He will not turn you away; He will, instead, offer answers that are tested and true. Your job is to ask, to listen, and to trust.

God Himself is what enlightens understanding about everything else in life. Knowledge about any subject is fragmentary without the enlightenment that comes from His relationship to it.

Beth Moore

PASSION FOR THE WORK

Whatever your hand finds to do,
do it with your might.

Ecclesiastes 9:10 NKJV

🔖 Have you discovered a life's work that excites you? Do you have a vocation or an avocation about which you are passionate? Have you discovered something that makes you want to hop out of bed in the morning and get to work? And does that "something" make the world—and *your* world—a better place? If so, thank God every day for that blessing.

If you have not yet discovered work that blesses you and your world, don't allow yourself to become discouraged. Instead, keep searching and keep trusting that with God's help, you can—and will—find a meaningful way to serve your neighbors *and* your God.

🔖 *Get absolutely enthralled with something. Throw yourself into it with abandon. Get out of yourself. Be somebody. Do something.*

Norman Vincent Peale

🔖 *Success or failure can be pretty well predicted by the degree to which the heart is fully in it.*

John Eldredge

FORGIVENESS AND SPIRITUAL GROWTH

*And be kind to one another, tenderhearted,
forgiving one another, just as God in Christ
forgave you.*

Ephesians 4:32 NKJV

Forgiveness is an exercise in spiritual growth: The more we forgive, the more we grow. Conversely, bitterness makes spiritual growth impossible: When our hearts are filled with resentment and anger, there is no room left for love.

As Christians, we can and should continue to grow in the love and the knowledge of our Savior as long as we live. When we cease to grow, either emotionally or spiritually, we do ourselves and our loved ones a profound disservice. But, if we study God's Word, if we obey His commandments, and if we live in the center of His will, we will not be "stagnant" believers; we will, instead, be growing Christians . . . and that's exactly what God wants for us to be.

Forgiveness is the final form of love.

Reinhold Niebuhr

The fire of anger, if not quenched by loving forgiveness, will spread and defile and destroy the work of God.

Warren Wiersbe

PERSEVERING FOR GOD

But thanks be to God, who gives us the victory
through our Lord Jesus Christ. Therefore,
my beloved brethren, be steadfast, immovable,
always abounding in the work of the Lord,
knowing that your labor is not in vain in the Lord.

1 Corinthians 15:57, 58 NKJV

🍃 In a world filled with roadblocks and stumbling blocks, we need strength, courage, and perseverance. And, as an example of perfect perseverance, we need look no further than Jesus Christ.

Jesus finished what He began. Despite the torture He endured, despite the shame of the cross, Jesus was steadfast in His faithfulness to God. We, too, must remain faithful, especially during times of hardship.

Perhaps you are in a hurry for God to reveal His plans for your life. If so, be forewarned: God operates on His own timetable, not yours. Sometimes, God may answer your prayers with silence, and when He does, you must patiently persevere. In times of trouble, you must remain steadfast and trust in the merciful goodness of your Heavenly Father. Whatever your problem, He can handle it. Your job is to keep persevering until He does.

🍃 *All rising to a great place is by a winding stair.*

Francis Bacon

THE HAND THAT HEALS

I have heard your prayer, I have seen your tears;
surely I will heal you.

2 Kings 20:5 NKJV

Are you concerned about your spiritual, physical, or emotional health? If so, there is a timeless source of comfort and assurance that is as near your bookshelf. That source is the Holy Bible.

God's Word has much to say about every aspect of your life, including your health. And, when you face concerns of any sort—including health-related challenges— God is with You. So trust your medical doctor to do his or her part, but place your ultimate trust in your benevolent Heavenly Father. His healing touch, like His love, endures forever.

God helps the sick in two ways, through the science of medicine and through the science of faith and prayer.

Norman Vincent Peale

Jesus Christ is the One by Whom, for Whom, through Whom everything was made. Therefore, He knows what's wrong in your life and how to fix it.

Anne Graham Lotz

SPEAKING WITH A VOICE OF TRIUMPH

Oh, clap your hands, all you peoples!
Shout to God with the voice of triumph!

Psalm 47:1 NKJV

❧ Are you living the triumphant life that God has promised? Or are you, instead, a spiritual shrinking violet? As you ponder that question, consider this: God does not intend that you live a life that is commonplace or mediocre. And He doesn't want you hide your light "under a basket." Instead, He wants you to "Let your light so shine before men, that they may see your good works and glorify your Father in heaven" (Matthew 5:16 NKJV). In short, God wants you to live a triumphant life so that others might know precisely what it means to be a believer.

The Christian life should be a triumphal celebration, a daily exercise in thanksgiving and praise. Join that celebration today. And while you're at it, make sure that you let others *know* that you've joined.

❧ *Being loved by Him whose opinion matters most gives us the security to risk loving, too—even loving ourselves.*

Gloria Gaither

A Fresh Start

I will give you a new heart
and put a new spirit within you

Ezekiel 36:26 NKJV

🌿 Each new day offers countless opportunities to serve God, to seek His will, and to obey His teachings. But each day also offers countless opportunities to stray from God's commandments and to wander far from His path.

Sometimes, we wander aimlessly in a wilderness of our own making, but God has better plans of us. And, whenever we ask Him to renew our strength and guide our steps, He does so.

Consider this day a new beginning. Consider it a fresh start, a renewed opportunity to serve your Creator with willing hands and a loving heart. Ask God to renew your sense of purpose as He guides your steps. Today is a glorious opportunity to serve God. Seize that opportunity while you can; tomorrow may indeed be too late.

🌿 *My spirit has become dry because it forgets to feed on You.*

John of the Cross

🌿 *Begin to be now what you will be hereafter.*

Jerome

The Size of Your Problems

*Ah, Lord God! Behold, You have made
the heavens and the earth by Your great power and
outstretched arm. There is nothing too hard for You.*

Jeremiah 32:17 NKJV

❧ If a temporary loss of perspective has left you worried, exhausted, or both, it's time to readjust your thought patterns. Negative thoughts are habit-forming; thankfully, so are positive ones. With practice, you can form the habit of focusing on God's priorities and *your* possibilities. When you do, you'll soon discover that you will spend less time fretting about your challenges and more time praising God for His gifts.

When you call upon the Lord and prayerfully seek His will, He will give you wisdom and perspective. When you make God's priorities your priorities, He will direct your steps and calm your fears. So today and every day hereafter, pray for a sense of balance and perspective. And remember: No problems are too big for God—and that includes yours.

❧ *How important it is for us—young and old—to live as if Jesus would return any day—to set our goals, make our choices, raise our children, and conduct business with the perspective of the imminent return of our Lord.*

Gloria Gaither

DOING THE RIGHT THING

*And you shall do what is right and good in the sight
of the Lord, that it may be well with you.*

Deuteronomy 6:18 NKJV

☙ Oswald Chambers, the author of the Christian
classic devotional text *My Utmost For His Highest*,
advised, "Never support an experience which does
not have God as its source, and faith in God as its
result." These words serve as a powerful reminder
that, as Christians, we are called to walk with God
and obey His commandments. But, we live in a
world that presents us with countless temptations
to stray far from God's path. We Christians, when
confronted with sin, have clear instructions: Walk—
or better yet run—in the opposite direction.

Today, take every step of your journey with God
as your traveling companion. Read His Word and
follow His commandments. Support only those
activities that further God's kingdom and your
spiritual growth. Be an example of righteous living
to your friends, to your neighbors, and to your
children. Then, reap the blessings that God has
promised to all those who live according to His
will and His Word.

☙ *Our progress in holiness depends on God and
ourselves—on God's grace and on our will to be holy.*

Mother Teresa

A HEART PREPARED FOR PRAYER

*And whenever you stand praying, if you have
anything against anyone, forgive him, that your Father
in heaven may also forgive you your trespasses.*

Mark 11:25 NKJV

🍃 Life is a patchwork of successes and failures,
victories and defeats, joys and sorrows. When
we experience life's inevitable disappointments,
we may become embittered, but God instructs us
to do otherwise. God understands the futility of
bitterness, and He knows that without forgiveness,
we can never enjoy the spiritual abundance that
He offers us through the person of His Son Jesus.

Christ's teachings are straightforward: Before
we offer our prayers to God, we should cleanse
ourselves of bitterness, hatred, jealousy, and regret.
When we do so, we can petition God with pure
hearts.

🍃 Be so preoccupied with good will that you haven't
room for ill will.

E. Stanley Jones

🍃 Forgiveness is the key that unlocks the door of
resentment and the handcuffs of hate. It is a power
that breaks the chains of bitterness and the shackles of
selfishness.

Corrie ten Boom

Wed

THE RICHES OF HIS GRACE

In Him we have redemption through His blood,
the forgiveness of sins, according to the riches of
His grace which He made to abound toward us
in all wisdom and prudence....

Ephesians 1:7, 8 NKJV

 We are saved, not by our own righteousness, but by God's grace. God's priceless gift of eternal life is not a reward for our good deeds; it is a manifestation of God's infinite love for those who worship Him and accept His Son as their Savior.

Are you absolutely certain that you have accepted the gift of salvation? If not, drop to your knees this very instant and accept Christ as your personal Savior. And, if you are already the thankful recipient of eternal life through Christ Jesus, use this day as an opportunity to share your testimony with friends and family members.

Jesus is the sovereign friend and ultimate savior of mankind. Christ showed enduring love for us by willingly sacrificing His own life so that we might have eternal life. Let us love Him, praise Him, and share His message of salvation with our neighbors and with the world.

 The Gospel is not so much a demand as it is an offer, an offer of new life to man by the grace of God.

E. Stanley Jones

MATERIAL AND SPIRITUAL POSSESSIONS

*For what will it profit a man if he gains
the whole world, and loses his own soul?
Or what will a man give in exchange for his soul?*

Mark 8:36, 37 NKJV

🔖 Earthly riches are temporary: here today and soon gone forever. Spiritual riches, on the other hand, are permanent: ours today, ours tomorrow, ours throughout eternity. Yet all too often, we focus our thoughts and energies on the accumulation of earthly treasures, leaving precious little time to accumulate the only treasures that really matter: the spiritual kind.

Our material possessions have the potential to do great good or terrible harm, depending upon how we choose to use them. As believers, our instructions are clear: We must use our possessions in accordance with God's commandments, and we must be faithful stewards of the gifts He has seen fit to bestow upon us.

Today, let us honor God by placing no other gods before Him. God comes first; everything else comes next—and "everything else" most certainly includes *all* of our earthly possessions.

🔖 *Hold everything earthly with a loose hand, but grasp eternal things with a deathlike grip.*

C. H. Spurgeon

AND THE GREATEST OF THESE

And now abide faith, hope, love, these three;
but the greatest of these is love.

1 Corinthians 13:13 NKJV

The familiar words of 1st Corinthians 13 remind us of the importance of love. Faith is important, of course. So too is hope. But love is more important still.

Christ showed His love for us on the cross, and, as Christians, we are called upon to return Christ's love by sharing it. We are commanded (not advised, not encouraged…commanded!) to love one another just as Christ loved us (John 13:34). That's a tall order, but as Christians, we are obligated to follow it.

Sometimes love is easy (puppies and sleeping children come to mind) and sometimes love is hard (fallible human beings come to mind). But God's Word is clear: We are to love our all our friends and neighbors, not just the lovable ones. So today, take time to spread Christ's message by word and by example. And the greatest of these is, of course, is example.

Carve your name on hearts, not on marble.

C. H. Spurgeon

A soul cannot live without loving. It must have something to love, for it was created to love.

Catherine of Siena

GOOD TREASURE FROM A GOOD HEART

A good man out of the good treasure of his heart brings forth good things, and an evil man out of the evil treasure brings forth evil things.

Matthew 12:35 NKJV

How can we demonstrate our love for God? By accepting His Son as our personal Savior and by placing Christ squarely at the center of our lives and our hearts. Jesus said that if we are to love Him, we must obey His commandments (John 14:15). Thus, our obedience to the Master is an expression of our love for Him.

In Ephesians 2:10 we read, "For we are His workmanship, created in Christ Jesus for good works." (NKJV). These words are instructive: We are not saved by good works, but for good works. Good works are not the root, but rather the fruit of our salvation.

Today, let the fruits of your stewardship be a clear demonstration of your love for Christ. When you do, your good heart will bring forth many good things for yourself and for God. Christ has given you spiritual abundance and eternal life. You, in turn, owe Him good treasure from a single obedient heart: yours.

Each one, according to his own ability, should be a patter of goodness to others.

Basil the Great

We Are All Teachers

Be gentle to all, able to teach, patient.

2 Timothy 2:24 NKJV

🌿 We are all teachers: All of us serve as powerful examples to young people, friends, and family members. And we must behave accordingly.

Daniel Webster wrote, "If we work in marble, it will perish; if we work upon brass, time will efface it; if we rear temples, they will crumble into dust; but if we work upon immortal minds and instill in them just principles, we are then engraving upon tablets which no time will efface, but which will brighten and brighten to all eternity." These words remind us of the glorious opportunities that are available to those of us who teach. May we, with God's help, touch the hearts and minds of those whom God has placed along our way. And, by doing so, may we refashion *this* wonderful world... and *the next*.

🌿 *Make it a rule, and pray to God to help you to keep it, never to lie down at night without being able to say: "I have made at least one human being a little wiser, a little happier, or a little better this day"*

Charles Kingsley

🌿 *Teaching is a divine calling. Whether we teach at home, at church, or in a school classroom, transfer of knowledge is a significant undertaking.*

Suzanne Dale Ezell

How Much Does God Deserve?

Freely you have received, freely give.

Matthew 10:8 NKJV

🌿 What does God deserve from you? Will you give Him the firstfruits of your harvest? Will you honor Him with the best you have to offer? Will you praise the Creator not only with your words but also with your deeds?

Every day is a fresh opportunity to honor God with your prayers, with your praise, with your deeds, and with your testimony. Your Heavenly Father deserves no less.

Does the level of your stewardship honor the One who has given you everything? If so, God will bless you because of your obedience. And if your stewardship has been somehow deficient, the best day to begin serving Him more faithfully is, of course, this one.

🌿 *I can usually sense that a leading is from the Holy Spirit when it calls me to humble myself, to serve somebody, to encourage somebody, or to give something away. Very rarely will the evil one lead us to do those kind of things.*

Bill Hybels

🌿 *How can we withhold from another what God has so generously allowed us to use and enjoy?*

Jan Winebrenner

DEMONSTRATING YOUR FAITH

*So brothers and sisters, be careful that none of you has
an evil, unbelieving heart that will turn you away from
the living God. But encourage each other every day
while it is "today." Help each other so none of you
will become hardened because sin has tricked you.*

Hebrews 3:13 NCV

In his second letter to Timothy, Paul offers a
message to believers of every generation when he
writes, "God has not given us a spirit of timidity"
(1:7). Paul's meaning is crystal clear: When sharing
our testimonies, we, as Christians, must be courageous, forthright, and unashamed.

We live in a world that desperately needs the
healing message of Christ Jesus. Every believer,
each in his or her own way, bears responsibility for
sharing the Good News of our Savior. It is important to remember that we bear testimony through
both words and actions. Wise Christians follow the
admonition of St. Francis of Assisi who advised,
"Preach the gospel at all times and, if necessary,
use words."

You know how Christ has touched your heart
and changed your life. Now is the time to share
your testimony with others. So today, preach the
Gospel through your words and your deeds...but
not necessarily in that order.

*Remember, a small light will do a great deal when it
is in a very dark place.*

D. L. Moody

The Daily Path

Then He said to them all, "If anyone desires to come after Me, let him deny himself, and take up his cross daily, and follow Me. For whoever desires to save his life will lose it, but whoever loses his life for My sake will save it."

Luke 9:23, 24 NKJV

There's an old saying—trite but true—"Today is the first day of the rest of your life." And whatever your situation may be, remember that this day holds boundless possibilities *if* you are wise enough and observant enough to claim them.

Christ came to this earth to give us abundant life and eternal salvation. Our task is to accept Christ's grace with joy in our hearts and praise on our lips. When we fashion our days around Jesus, we are transformed: We see the world differently, we act differently, and we feel differently about ourselves and our neighbors. We face the inevitable challenges and disappointments of each day armed with the joy of Christ and the promise of salvation.

So whatever this day holds for you, begin it and end it with God as your partner and Christ as your Savior. And throughout the day, give thanks to the One who created you and saved you. God's love for you is infinite. Accept it joyously and be thankful.

With each new dawn, life delivers a package to your front door, rings your doorbell, and runs.

Charles Swindoll

EXPECTING THE IMPOSSIBLE

Is anything too hard for the Lord?

Genesis 18:14 NKJV

🖎 Do you believe that God is at work in the world? And do you also believe that nothing is impossible for Him? If so, then you also believe that God is perfectly capable of doing things that you, as a mere human being with limited vision and limited understanding, would deem to be utterly impossible. And that's precisely what God does.

Since He created our universe out of nothingness, God has made a habit of doing miraculous things. And He still works miracles today. Expect Him to work miracles in your own life, and then be watchful. With God, absolutely nothing is impossible, including an amazing assortment of miracles that He stands ready, willing, and able to perform for you and yours.

🖎 *If all things are possible with God, then all things are possible to him who believes in him.*

Corrie ten Boom

🖎 *Start by doing what's necessary, then what's possible, and suddenly you're doing the impossible.*

Francis of Assisi

🖎 *When you ask God to do something, don't ask timidly; put your whole heart into it.*

Marie T. Freeman

THE JOYS OF A CLEAR CONSCIENCE

*Let us come near to God with a sincere heart
and a sure faith, because we have been made free
from a guilty conscience, and our bodies
have been washed with pure water.*

Hebrews 10:22 NCV

🍂 Few things in life torment us more than the pangs of a guilty conscience. And, few things in life provide more contentment than the knowledge that we are obeying God's commandments.

A clear conscience is one of the rewards we earn when we obey God's Word and follow His will. When we follow God's will and accept His gift of salvation, our earthly rewards are never-ceasing, and our heavenly rewards are everlasting.

🍂 *Sweet shall be your rest if your heart does not reproach you.*

Thomas à Kempis

🍂 *Christian joy is a gift from God flowing from a good conscience.*

Philip Neri

🍂 *A good conscience is a continual feast.*

Francis Bacon

IN SEARCH OF ANSWERS

And you will seek Me and find Me,
when you search for Me with all your heart.

Jeremiah 29:13 NKJV

❧ You've got questions? God's got answers. And if you'd like to hear from Him, here's precisely what you must do: Petition Him with a sincere heart; be still; be patient; and listen. Then, in His own time and in His own fashion, God will answer you questions and give you guidance for the journey ahead.

Today, turn over everything to your Creator. Pray constantly about matters great and small. Seek God's instruction and His direction. And remember: God hears your prayers and answers them. But He won't answer the prayers that you don't get around to praying. So pray early and often. And then wait patiently for answers that are sure to come.

❧ *Nothing is clearer than that prayer has its only worth and significance in the great fact that God hears and answers prayer.*

E. M. Bounds

❧ *I live in the spirit of prayer; I pray as I walk, when I lie down, and when I rise. And, the answers are always coming.*

George Mueller

WHEN WE ARE BLESSED, WE ARE TESTED

Blessed is the man who walks not in the counsel of the ungodly, nor stands in the path of sinners, nor sits in the seat of the scornful.

Psalm 1:1 NKJV

🍃 Sometimes, we are tested more in times of plenty than we are in times of privation. When we experience life's difficult days, we may be more likely to turn our thoughts and hearts to God. But in times of plenty, when the sun is shining and our minds are at ease, we may be tempted to believe that our good fortune is entirely of our own making. Nothing could be further from the truth. God plays a hand in every aspect of everyday life, and for the blessings that we receive, we must offer thanks and praise to Him, not to ourselves.

Have you been blessed by God? Are you enjoying the abundance He has promised? If so, praise Him for His gifts. Praise Him faithfully and humbly. And don't, for a single moment, allow a prideful heart to separate you from blessings of your loving Father.

🍃 *Blessings can either humble us and draw us closer to God or allow us to become full of pride and self-sufficiency.*

Jim Cymbala

mon

DABBLERS BEWARE

*There is one thing I always do. Forgetting the past
and straining toward what is ahead, I keep trying
to reach the goal and get the prize for which
God called me . . . .*

Philippians 3:13, 14 NKJV

❧ Is Christ the focus of your life? Are you fired with enthusiasm for Him? Are you an energized Christian who allows God's Son to reign over every aspect of your day? Make no mistake: That's exactly what God intends for you to do.

God has given you the gift of eternal life through His Son. In response to God's priceless gift, you are instructed to focus your thoughts, your prayers, and your energies upon God and His only begotten Son. To do so, you must resist the subtle yet powerful temptation to become a "spiritual dabbler."

A person who dabbles in the Christian faith is unwilling to place God in His rightful place: above all other things. Resist that temptation; make God the cornerstone and the touchstone of your life. When you do, He will give you all the strength and wisdom you need to live victoriously for Him.

❧ *Give me the person who says, "This one thing I do, and not these fifty things I dabble in."*

D. L. Moody

HOW OFTEN DO YOU ASK?

*Ask, and it will be given to you; seek,
and you will find; knock, and it will be opened to you.
For everyone who asks receives, and he who seeks
finds, and to him who knocks it will be opened.*

Matthew 7:7, 8 NKJV

How often do you ask for God's help? Occasionally? Intermittently? Whenever you experience a crisis? Hopefully not. Hopefully, you have developed the habit of asking for God's assistance early and often. And hopefully, you have learned to seek His guidance in every aspect of your life.

God has promised that when you ask for His help, He will not withhold it. So ask. Ask Him to meet the needs of your day. Ask Him for wisdom. Ask Him to lead you, to protect you, and to correct you. And trust the answers He gives.

God stands at the door and waits. When you knock on His door, He answers. Your task, of course, is to seek His guidance prayerfully, confidently, and often.

Aspire to God with short but frequent outpourings of the heart; admire His bounty; invoke His aid; cast yourself in spirit at the foot of His cross; adore His goodness; treat with Him of your salvation; give Him your whole soul a thousand times in the day.

Francis of Sales

PREPARING FOR LIFE . . . AND DEATH

For to me, to live is Christ, and to die is gain.

Philippians 1:21 NKJV

&- God has given you the gift of life. How will you use that gift? Will you allow God's Son to reign over your heart? And will you treat each day as a precious treasure from your Heavenly Father? You should, and, hopefully, you will.

Every day that we live, we should be preparing to die. If we seek to live purposeful, productive lives, we will be ever mindful that our time here on earth is limited, and we will conduct ourselves accordingly.

Life is a glorious opportunity, but it is also shockingly brief. We must serve God each day as if it were our last day. When we do, we prepare ourselves for the inevitable end of life on here earth, and or the victory that is certain to follow.

&- *It ought to be the business of every day to prepare for our last day.*

Matthew Henry

&- *Take care of your life and the Lord will take care of your death.*

George Whitefield

KEEPING UP WITH THE JONESES . . . OR NOT!

A sound heart is life to the body,
but envy is rottenness to the bones.

Proverbs 14:30 NKJV

As a member in good standing of this highly competitive, 21st-century world, you know that the demands and expectations of everyday living can seem burdensome, even overwhelming at times. Keeping up with the Joneses can become a fulltime job if you let it. A better strategy, of course, is to stop trying to please the neighbors and to concentrate, instead, upon pleasing God.

Perhaps you have set your goals high; if so, congratulations! You're willing to dream big dreams, and that's a very good thing. But as you consider your life's purpose, don't allow your quest for excellence to interfere with the spiritual journey that God has planned for you.

As a believer, your instructions are clear: You must strive to please God. How do you please Him? By accepting His Son and obeying His commandments. All other concerns—including, but not limited to, keeping up with the Joneses— are of little or no importance.

Theirs is an endless road, a hopeless maze, who seek for goods before they seek for God.

Bernard of Clairvaux

FINDING (AND TRUSTING) MENTORS

*A wise man will hear and increase learning,
and a man of understanding will attain wise counsel.*

Proverbs 1:5 NKJV

🍃 Do you seek to become wise? Then you must acknowledge that you are not wise enough *on your own*. When you face an important decision, you must first study God's Word, and you should also seek the counsel of trusted friends and mentors.

When we arrive at the inevitable crossroads of life, God inevitably sends righteous men and women to guide us *if we let them*. If we are willing to listen and to learn, then we, too, will become wise. And God will bless our endeavors.

🍃 *Do not open your heart to every man, but discuss your affairs with one who is wise and who fears God.*

Thomas à Kempis

🍃 *The next best thing to being wise oneself is to live in a circle of those who are.*

C. S. Lewis

🍃 *It takes a wise person to give good advice, but an even wiser person to take it.*

Marie T. Freeman

WHEN THE BOSS ISN'T WATCHING

Go to the ant, you sluggard! Consider her ways and be wise, which, having no captain, overseer or ruler, provides her supplies in the summer, and gathers her food in the harvest. How long will you slumber, O sluggard? When will you rise from your sleep?

Proverbs 6:6–9 NKJV

🌿 The Bible instructs us that we can learn an important lesson of a surprising source: ants. Ants are among nature's most industrious creatures. They do their work without supervision and without hesitation. We should do likewise.

God's Word is clear: We are instructed to work diligently and faithfully. We are told that the fields are ripe for the harvest, that the workers are few, and that the importance of our work is profound. Let us labor, then, for our Master without hesitation and without complaint. Nighttime is coming. Until it does, let us honor our Heavenly Father with grateful hearts and willing hands.

🌿 *There is a silent dignity, a fundamental usefulness, and a primeval necessity in work.*

Father Flanagan

🌿 *No horse gets anywhere until he is harnessed. No life ever grows great until it is focused, dedicated, disciplined.*

Harry Emerson Fosdick

Sun

DEPENDING UPON GOD

Depend on the Lord and his strength; always go to him for help. Remember the miracles he has done; remember his wonders and his decisions.

Psalm 105:4, 5 NCV

🌿 God is a never-ending source of strength and courage if we call upon Him. When we are weary, He gives us strength. When we see no hope, God reminds us of His promises. When we grieve, God wipes away our tears.

Do you feel overwhelmed by today's responsibilities? Do you feel pressured by the ever-increasing demands of 21st-century life? Then turn your concerns and your prayers over to God. He knows your needs, and He has promised to meet those needs. Whatever your circumstances, God will protect you and care for you...*if* you let Him. Invite Him into your heart and allow Him to renew you spirits. When you trust Him and Him alone, He will never fail you.

🌿 *There are two things we are called to do: we are to depend on His strength and be obedient to His Word. If we can't handle being dependent and obedient, we will never become the kind of people who have a heart for God.*

Stuart Briscoe

SPIRITUAL WEALTH

He who trusts in his riches will fall,
but the righteous will flourish . . . .

Proverbs 11:28 NKJV

&- Your material possessions are completely, utterly, and indisputably temporary. Every possession that you own will pass away, and soon. Thankfully, your spiritual possessions are not so fragile.

When you welcomed Christ into your heart, God promised that you would receive the gift of eternal life. The implications of that gift are beyond human understanding, but what you *can* understand is this: Material wealth is inconsequential when compared to God's spiritual gifts.

&- *All those who look to draw their satisfaction from the wells of the world will soon be thirsty again!*

Anne Graham Lotz

&- *Our soul can never have rest in things that are beneath itself.*

Juliana of Norwich

&- *If the glories of heaven were more real to us, if we lived less for material things and more for things eternal and spiritual, we would be less easily disturbed in this present life.*

Billy Graham

LAUGHING WITH LIFE

A merry heart makes a cheerful countenance....

Proverbs 15:13 NKJV

✦ Laughter is medicine for the soul, but sometimes, amid the stresses of the day, we forget to take our medicine. Instead of viewing our world with a mixture of optimism and humor, we allow worries and distractions to rob us of the joy that God intends for our lives.

The next time you find yourself dwelling upon the negatives of life, refocus your attention to things positive. The next time you find yourself falling prey to the blight of pessimism, stop yourself and turn your thoughts around. And, if you see your glass as "half-empty," rest assured that your spiritual vision is impaired. With God, your glass is never half empty. With God as your Protector and Christ as your Savior, your glass is filled to the brim and overflowing...forever.

Today, as you go about your daily activities, approach life with a smile on your lips and hope in your heart. And laugh every chance you get. After all, God created laughter for a reason...and Father indeed knows best. So laugh!

✦ *I think everybody ought to be a laughing Christian. I'm convinced that there's just one place where there's not any laughter, and that's hell.*

Jerry Clower

WHEN WE DON'T UNDERSTAND

*Now we see a dim reflection, as if we were looking
into a mirror, but then we shall see clearly.
Now I know only a part, but then I will know fully,
as God has known me.*

1 Corinthians 13:12 NCV

  ✍ As humans with limited understanding, we can never fully comprehend the hand of God. But as believers in a benevolent God, we must always trust the heart of our Heavenly Father.

  Before His crucifixion, Jesus went to the Mount of Olives and poured out His heart to God (Luke 22). Jesus knew of the agony that He was destined to endure, but He also knew that God's will must be done. We, like our Savior, face trials that bring fear and trembling to the very depths of our souls, but like Christ, we, too, must ultimately seek God's will, not our own.

  As this day unfolds, seek God's will for your own life and obey His Word. When you entrust your life to Him completely and without reservation, He will give you the strength to meet any challenge, the courage to face any trial, and the wisdom to live in His righteousness and in His peace.

  ✍ *A religion that is small enough for our understanding would not be big enough for our needs.*

Corrie ten Boom

FAITH-FILLED CHRISTIAN

*Give your worries to the Lord, and he will
take care of you. He will never let good people down.*

Psalm 55:22 NCV

Pessimism and Christianity don't mix. Why? Because Christians have every reason to be optimistic about life here on earth *and* life eternal. As C. H. Spurgeon observed, "Our hope in Christ for the future is the mainstream of our joy." But sometimes, we fall prey to worry, frustration, anxiety, or sheer exhaustion, and our hearts become heavy. What's needed is plenty of rest, a large dose of perspective, and God's healing touch, but not necessarily in that order.

Today, make this promise to yourself and keep it: Vow to be a hope-filled Christian. Think optimistically about your life, your profession, your future, and your students. Trust your hopes, not your fears. Take time to celebrate God's glorious creation. And then, when you've filled your heart with hope and gladness, share your optimism with others. They'll be better for it, and so will you. But not necessarily in that order.

*Never yield to gloomy anticipation. Place your hope
and confidence in God. He has no record of failure.*

Mrs. Charles E. Cowman

WHATEVER IT IS, GOD IS BIGGER

But Jesus turned around, and when He saw her
He said, "Be of good cheer, daughter; your faith
has made you well." And the woman
was made well from that hour.

Matthew 9:22 NKJV

✤ Genuine faith is never meant to be locked up in the heart of a believer; to the contrary, it is meant to be shared with the world. But, if you sincerely seek to share your faith, you must first find it.

When a suffering woman sought healing by merely touching the hem of His cloak, Jesus replied, " Be of good cheer, daughter; your faith has made you well." (Matthew 9:22 NKJV). The message to believers of every generation is clear: Live by faith today and every day.

How can you strengthen your faith? Through praise, through worship, through Bible study, and through prayer. And, as your faith becomes stronger, you will find ways to share it with your friends, your family, and with the world. When you place your faith, your trust, indeed your life it the hands of Christ Jesus, you'll be amazed at the marvelous things He can do with you and through you; so trust God's plans. With Him, all things are possible, and whatever "it" is, God is bigger.

✤ *Faith is a strong power, mastering any difficulty in the strength of the Lord who made heaven and earth.*

Corrie ten Boom

TODAY IS YOUR CLASSROOM

If you teach the wise, they will get knowledge.

Proverbs 21:11 NCV

Today is your classroom: What will you learn? Will you use today's experiences as tools for personal growth, or will you ignore the lessons that life and God are trying to teach you? Will you carefully study God's Word, and will you apply His teachings to the experiences of everyday life? The events of today have much to teach. You have much to learn. May you live—and learn—accordingly.

The wonderful thing about God's schoolroom is that we get to grade our own papers. You see, He doesn't test us so He can learn how well we're doing. He tests us so we can discover how well we're doing.

Charles Swindoll

Don't let circumstances distress you. Rather, look for the will of God for your life to be revealed in and through those circumstances.

Billy Graham

God's plan for our guidance is for us to grow gradually in wisdom before we get to the crossroads.

Bill Hybels

MIDCOURSE CORRECTIONS

O Lord my God, in You I put my trust; save me from all those who persecute me; and deliver me . . . .

Psalm 7:1 NKJV

❧ In our fast-paced world, everyday life has become an exercise in managing change. Our circumstances change; our relationships change; our bodies change. We grow older every day, as does our world. Thankfully, God does not change. He is eternal, as are the truths that are found in His Holy Word.

Are you facing one of life's inevitable "midcourse corrections"? If so, you must place your faith, your trust, and your life in the hands of the One who does not change: your Heavenly Father. He is the unmoving rock upon which you must construct this day and every day. When you do, you are secure.

❧ *Wise people listen to wise instruction, especially instruction from the Word of God.*

Warren Wiersbe

❧ *The God who orchestrates the universe has a good many things to consider that have not occurred to me, and it is well that I leave them to Him.*

Elisabeth Elliot

❧ *The Rock of Ages is the great sheltering encirclement.*

Oswald Chambers

more

GOD'S SURPRISING PLANS

But as it is written: "Eye has not seen, nor ear heard,
nor have entered into the heart of man the things
which God has prepared for those who love Him."
1 Corinthians 2:9 NKJV

🖋 God has plans for your life, wonderful, surprising plans…but He won't force those plans upon you. To the contrary, He has given you free will, the ability to make decisions on your own. With that freedom to choose comes the responsibility of living with the consequences of the choices you make.

If you seek to live in accordance with God's will for your life—and you should—then you will live in accordance with His commandments. You will study God's Word, and you will be watchful for His signs. You will associate with fellow Christians who will encourage your spiritual growth, and you will listen to that inner voice that speaks to you in the quiet moments of your daily devotionals.

God intends to use you in wonderful, unexpected ways if you let Him. The decision to seek God's plan and to follow it is yours and yours alone. The consequences of that decision have implications that are both profound and eternal, so choose carefully.

🖋 _Even when we cannot see the why and wherefore_
of God's dealings, we know that there is love in and
behind them, so we can rejoice always.

J. I. Packer

TODAY: A DAY FOR CELEBRATION

Rejoice in the Lord always. Again I will say, rejoice!
                                        Philippians 4:4 NKJV

🌿 Oswald Chambers correctly observed, "Joy is the great note all throughout the Bible." C. S. Lewis echoed that thought when he wrote, "Joy is the serious business of heaven." But, even the most dedicated Christians can, on occasion, forget to celebrate each day for what it is: a priceless gift from God.

Today, let us be joyful Christians with smiles on our faces and kind words on our lips. After all, this is God's day, and He has given us clear instructions for its use. We are commanded to rejoice and be glad. So, with no further ado, let the celebration begin....

🌿 *All our life is a celebration for us; we are convinced, in fact, that God is always everywhere. We sing while we work...we pray while we carry out all life's other occupations.*
                                        Clement of Alexandria

🌿 *The church is the last place on earth to be solemn... provided you have lived right.*
                                        Sam Jones

🌿 *Joy comes not from what we have but from what we are.*
                                        C. H. Spurgeon

Wed

GOD'S WISDOM:
AN ENDLESS FOUNTAIN

*Understanding is like a fountain which gives life
to those who use it.*

Proverbs 16:22 NCV

✑ Wisdom is like a savings account: If you add to it consistently, then eventually you will have accumulated a great sum. The secret to success is consistency.

Do you seek wisdom for yourself and for your family? Then you must keep learning, and you must keep motivating them to do likewise. The ultimate source of wisdom, of course, is the Word of God. When you study God's Word and live according to His commandments, you will accumulate wisdom day by day. And finally, with God's help, you'll have enough wisdom to keep *and* enough left over to share.

✑ *Most of us go through life praying a little, planning a little, jockeying for position, hoping but never being quite certain of anything, and always secretly afraid that we will miss the way. This is a tragic waste of truth and never gives rest to the heart. There is a better way. It is to repudiate our own wisdom and take instead the infinite wisdom of God.*

A. W. Tozer

MAKING ALL THINGS NEW

*The One who was sitting on the throne said, "Look!
I am making everything new!" Then he said, "Write
this, because these words are true and can be trusted."*
Revelation 21:5 NCV

🔖 Sometimes, the demands of everyday life can
drain us of our strength and rob us of the joy that
is rightfully ours in Christ. When we find ourselves
tired, discouraged, or worse, there is a source from
which we can draw the power needed to renew
our spirits. That source is God. Our Heavenly
Father intends that we lead joyous lives filled with
abundance and peace. But sometimes, abundance
and peace seem very far away. It is then that we
must turn to God for renewal, and when we do, He
will restore us.

Are you tired or troubled? Turn your heart
toward God in prayer. Are you weak or worried?
Take the time to delve deeply into God's Holy
Word. Are you spiritually depleted? Call upon
fellow believers to support you, and call upon
Christ to renew your spirit and your life. When you
do, you'll discover that the Creator of the universe
stands always ready and always able to create a new
sense of wonderment and joy in you.

🔖 *The amazing thing about Jesus is that He doesn't just
patch up our lives, He gives us a brand new sheet, a
clean slate to start over, all new.*

Gloria Gaither

THE PROBLEM OF SIN

*Watch and pray so that you will not fall
into temptation. The spirit is willing
but the body is weak.*

Matthew 26:41 NIV

After fasting forty days and nights in the desert, Jesus was tempted by Satan. Christ used scripture to rebuke the devil. (Matthew 4:1–11) We must do likewise. The Holy Bible provides us with a perfect blueprint for righteous living. If we consult that blueprint daily and follow it carefully, we build our lives according to God's plan.

We live in a world that is brimming with opportunities to stray from God's will. Ours is a society filled with temptations, a place where it is all too easy to disobey God. We, like our Savior, must guard ourselves against these temptations. We do so, in part, through prayer and through a careful reading of God's Word.

The battle against Satan is ongoing. Be vigilant, and call upon your Heavenly Father to protect you. When you petition Him with a sincere heart, God will be your shield, now and forever.

Rebuke the Enemy in your own name and he laughs; command him in the name of Christ and he flees.

John Eldredge

YOUR TO-DO LIST . . . AND GOD'S

Come near to God, and God will come near to you.
You sinners, clean sin out of your lives. You who are
trying to follow God and the world at the same time,
make your thinking pure.

James 4:8 NCV

❧ Have you fervently asked God to help prioritize Your life? Have you asked Him for guidance and for the courage to do the things that you know need to be done? If so, then you're continually inviting your Creator to reveal Himself in a variety of ways. As a follower of Christ, you must do no less.

When you make God's priorities your priorities, you will receive God's abundance and His peace. When you make God a full partner in every aspect of your life, He will lead you along the proper path: His path. When you allow God to reign over your heart, He will honor you with spiritual blessings that are simply too numerous to count. So, as you plan for the day ahead, make God's will your ultimate priority. When you do, every other priority will have a tendency to fall neatly into place.

❧ *With God, it's never "Plan B" or "second best."*
It's always "Plan A." And, if we let Him, He'll make
something beautiful of our lives.

Gloria Gaither

FINDING COMFORT

I was very worried, but you comforted me . . . .

Psalms 94:19 NCV

❧ If you are a person with lots of obligations and plenty of responsibilities, it is simply a fact of life: You worry. From time to time, you worry about health, about finances, about safety, about family, and about countless other concerns, some great and some small.

Where is the best place to take your worries? Take them to God. Take your troubles to Him; take your fears to Him; take your doubts to Him; take your weaknesses to Him; take your sorrows to Him . . . and leave them all there. Seek protection from the One who offers you eternal salvation; build your spiritual house upon the Rock that cannot be moved.

❧ *Give your cares to Him who cares for the flowers of the field. Rest assured He will also care for you.*

C. H. Spurgeon

❧ *I have a better Caretaker. He it is who lies in a manger but at the same time sits at the right hand of God, the almighty Father. Therefore be at rest.*

Martin Luther, in a letter to his wife Kate,
eleven days before his death.

A POWER BEYOND UNDERSTANDING

I pray also that you will have greater understanding in your heart so you will know the hope to which he has called us and that you will know how rich and glorious are the blessings God has promised his holy people. And you will know that God's power is very great for us who believe.

Ephesians 1:18, 19 NCV

❧ Ours is a God of infinite possibilities. But sometimes, because of our limited faith and limited understanding, we wrongly assume that God cannot or will not intervene in the affairs of mankind. Such assumptions are simply wrong.

Are you afraid to ask God to do big things in your life? Is your faith threadbare and worn? If so, it's time to abandon your doubts and reclaim your faith in God's promises.

God's Holy Word makes it clear: Absolutely nothing is impossible for the Lord. And since the Bible means what it says, you can be comforted in the knowledge that the Creator of the universe can do miraculous things in your own life and in the lives of your loved ones. Your challenge, as a believer, is to take God at His Word, and to expect the miraculous.

❧ *He upholds the whole creation. What cannot he do for us, far beyond our conception and expectation, He who hangs the earth upon nothing?*

Matthew Henry

THE WISDOM OF KINDNESS

Kind people do themselves a favor,
but cruel people bring trouble on themselves.

Proverbs 11:17 NCV

✤ If we believe the words of Proverbs 11:17—and we should—then we understand that kindness is its own reward. And, if we to obey the commandments of our Savior—and we should—we must sow seeds of kindness wherever we go.

Kindness, compassion, and forgiveness are hallmarks of our Christian faith. So today, in honor of the One who first showed compassion for us, let's teach our families and friends the art of kindness through our words *and* through our deeds. Our loved ones are watching…and so is God.

✤ *No one heals himself by wounding another.*

Ambrose of Milan

✤ *He who sows courtesy reaps friendship, and he who plants kindness gathers love.*

Basil the Great

✤ *Our lives, we are told, are but fleeting at best, like roses they fade and decay; then let us do good while the present is ours, be useful as long as we stay.*

Fanny Crosby

OBEDIENCE AND PRAISE

Praise the Lord! Happy are those who respect
the Lord, who want what he commands.

Psalms 112:1 NCV

❧ Psalm 112 links two powerful principles: obedience and praise. One of the most important ways that we can praise God is by obeying Him. As believers who have been saved by a risen Christ, we must worship our Creator, not only with our prayers and our words, but also with our actions.

Are you grateful for God's glorious gifts? Are you thankful for the treasure of eternal life that is yours through the sacrifice of God's Son Jesus? Of course you are. And one of the very best ways to express your gratitude to God is through obedience to the unchanging commandments of His Holy Word.

❧ *It is God's will that everything he has made should offer him glory.*

John of Carpathos

❧ *When you suffer and lose, that does not mean you are being disobedient to God. In fact, it might mean you're right in the center of His will. The path of obedience is often marked by times of suffering and loss.*

Charles Swindoll

❧ *God desires the least degree of obedience and submissiveness more than all those services you think of rendering Him.*

John of the Cross

CLAIMING CONTENTMENT IN A DISCONTENTED WORLD

Serving God does make us very rich,
if we are satisfied with what we have.

1 Timothy 6:6 NCV

❧ The world readily offers us many things, but lasting contentment is not one of them. Genuine contentment cannot be found in material possessions, earthly power, human relationships, or transitory fame. Genuine contentment starts God and His only begotten Son . . . and ends there.

Do you seek the contentment and peace that only God can offer? Then welcome His Son into your heart. Allow Christ to rule over every aspect of your day: talk with Him; walk with Him; be with Him; praise Him. When you do, you will discover the peace and contentment that only God can give.

❧ *What a shame it will be if those who have the grace of God within them should fall short of the contentment which worldly men have attained.*

C. H. Spurgeon

❧ *True contentment is a real and active virtue—not only affirmative but creative. It is the power of getting out of any situation all there is in it.*

G. K Chesterton

WALKING IN THE LIGHT

Then Jesus spoke to them again, saying,
"I am the light of the world. He who follows Me
shall not walk in darkness, but have the light of life."
John 8:12 NKJV

✤ God's Holy Word instructs us that Jesus is, "the way, the truth, and the life" (John 14:6, 7). Without Christ, we are as far removed from salvation as the east is removed from the west. And without Christ, we can never know the ultimate truth: God's truth.

Truth is God's way: He commands His believers live in truth, and He rewards those who do so. Jesus is the personification of God's liberating truth, a truth that offers salvation to mankind.

Do you seek to walk with God? Do you seek to feel His presence and His peace? Then you must walk in truth; you must walk in the light; you must walk with the Savior. There is simply no other way.

✤ *Jesus differs from all other teachers; they reach the ear, but he instructs the heart; they deal with the outward letter, but he imparts an inward taste for the truth.*

C. H. Spurgeon

✤ *Only Jesus Christ is the truth for everyone who has ever been born into the human race, regardless of culture, age, nationality, generation, heritage, gender, color, or language.*

Anne Graham Lotz

THE HEALING TOUCH
OF THE MASTER'S HAND

Those who sow in tears shall reap in joy.

Psalm 126:5 NKJV

🕊 Grief visits all of us who live long and love deeply. When we lose a loved one, or when we experience any other profound loss, darkness overwhelms us for a while, and it seems as if we cannot summon the strength to face another day—but, with God's help, we can.

When our friends or family members encounter life-shattering events, we struggle to find words that might offer them comfort and support. But finding the right words can be difficult, if not impossible. Sometimes, all that we can do is to be with our loved ones, offering them few words but much love.

Thankfully, God promises that He is "near to those who have a broken heart" (Psalm 34:18 NKJV). In times of intense sadness, we must turn to Him, and we must encourage our friends and family members to do likewise. When we do, our Father comforts us and, in time, He heals us.

🕊 *One of the more significant things God will bring out of our grief and depression is an ability to walk constructively with others through theirs. In fact, one of the purposes of God's comfort is to equip us to comfort others.*

David B. Biebel

PROSPEROUS GENEROSITY

The generous soul will be made rich,
and he who waters will also be watered himself.

Proverbs 11:25 NKJV

⚘ God rewards generosity just as surely as He punishes sin. If we become "generous souls" in the service of our Lord, God blesses us in ways that we cannot fully understand. But if we allow ourselves to become closefisted and miserly, either with our possessions *or* with our love, we deprive ourselves of the spiritual abundance that would otherwise be ours.

Do you seek God's abundance and His peace? Then share the blessings that God has given you. Share your possessions, share your faith, share your testimony, and share your love. God expects no less, and He deserves no less. And neither, come to think of it, do your neighbors.

⚘ We must not only give what we have, we must also give what we are.

Désiré Joseph Mercier

⚘ If you want to be truly happy, you won't find it on an endless quest for more stuff. You'll find it in receiving God generosity and the passing that generosity along.

Bill Hybels

A STEADFAST FAITH IN A STEADFAST GOD

I have set the Lord always before me;
because He is at my right hand I shall not be moved.

Psalms 16:8 NKJV

❧ God is faithful to us even when we are not faithful to Him. God keeps His promises to us even when we stray far from His will. He continues to love us even when we disobey His commandments. But God does not force His blessings upon us. If we are to experience His love and His grace, we must claim them for ourselves.

Are you tired, discouraged or fearful? Be comforted: God is with you. Are you confused? Listen to the quiet voice of your Heavenly Father. Are you bitter? Talk with God and seek His guidance. Are you celebrating a great victory? Thank God and praise Him. He is the Giver of all things good.

In whatever condition you find yourself, wherever you are, whether you are happy or sad, victorious or vanquished, troubled or triumphant, remember that God is faithful and that His love is eternal. And be comforted. God is not just near. He is here.

❧ *I have a great need for Christ; I have a great Christ for my need.*

C. H. Spurgeon

USING YOUR GIFTS TO SERVE

*There are different kinds of gifts, but they are all
from the same Spirit. There are different ways
to serve but the same Lord to serve.*

1 Corinthians 12:4, 5 NCV

❧ God gives each of us a unique assortment of
talents and opportunities. And our Heavenly
Father instructs us to be faithful stewards of the
gifts that He bestows upon us. But we live in a
world that encourages us to do otherwise.

Ours is a society that is filled to the brim with
countless opportunities to squander our time, our
resources, and our talents. So we must be watchful
for distractions and temptations that might lead us
astray.

God has blessed you with unique opportunities
to serve Him, and He has given you every tool that
you need to do so. Today, accept this challenge:
Value the talent that God has given you, nourish
it, make it grow, and share it with the world. After
all, the best way to say "Thank You" for God's gifts
is to use them.

❧ *If the attitude of servanthood is learned, by attending
to God as Lord. Then, serving others will develop as a
very natural way of life.*

Eugene Peterson

FORGIVENESS IS A FORM OF WISDOM

The discretion of a man makes him slow to anger,
and his glory is to overlook a transgression.

Proverbs 19:11 NCV

Bitterness is a form of self-punishment; forgiveness is a means of self-liberation. Bitterness focuses on the injustices of the past; forgiveness focuses on the blessings of the present and the opportunities of the future. Bitterness is an emotion that destroys you; forgiveness is a decision that empowers you. Bitterness is folly; forgiveness is wisdom.

If we call upon the Lord and seek to see the world as He sees it, our Heavenly Father gives us wisdom. When we make God's priorities our priorities, He will lead us according to His plan and according to His commandments. When we study God's Word, we are reminded that God's reality is the ultimate reality. May we live—and forgive—accordingly.

Wisdom is knowing what to overlook.

William James

God's heart of mercy provides for us not only pardon from sin but also a daily provision of spiritual food to strengthen us.

Jim Cymbala

CELEBRATING GOD'S HANDIWORK

The heavens declare the glory of God;
and the firmament shows His handiwork.

Psalm 19:1 NKJV

❧ When we consider God's glorious universe, we marvel at the miracle of nature. The smallest seedlings and grandest stars are all part of God's infinite creation. God has placed His handiwork on display for all to see, and if we are wise, we will make time each day to celebrate the world that surrounds us.

Today, as you fulfill the demands of everyday life, pause to consider the majesty of heaven and earth. It is as miraculous as it is beautiful, as incomprehensible as it is breathtaking.

The Psalmist reminds us that the heavens are a declaration of God's glory. May we never cease to praise the Father for a universe that stands as an awesome testimony to His presence and His power.

❧ *If there is anyone who is not enlightened by this sublime magnificence of created things, his is blind. If there is anyone who, seeing all these works of God, does not praise Him, he is dumb; if there is anyone who, from so many signs, cannot perceive God, that man is foolish.*

Bonaventure

TAPPING INTO GOD'S STRENGTH

For the eyes of the Lord are on the righteous,
and His ears are open to their prayers;
but the face of the Lord is against those who do evil.

1 Peter 3:12 NKJV

❧ Have you made God the cornerstone of your life, or is He relegated to a few hours on Sunday morning? Have you genuinely allowed God to reign over every corner of your heart, or have you attempted to place Him in a spiritual compartment? The answer to these questions will determine the direction of your day and your life.

God loves you. In times of trouble, He will comfort you; in times of sorrow, He will dry your tears. When you are or weak or sorrowful, God is as near as your next breath. He stands at the door of your heart and waits. Welcome Him in and allow Him to rule. And then, accept the peace, and the strength, and the protection, and the abundance that only God can give.

❧ *God can do all that we need.*

Juliana of Norwich

❧ *God is great and God is powerful, but we must invite him to be powerful in our lives. His strength is always there, but it's up to us to provide a channel through which that power can flow.*

Bill Hybels

WALKING WITH THE WISE

He who walks with wise men will be wise,
but the companion of fools will be destroyed.

Proverbs 13:20 NKJV

❧ Do you wish to become wise? Then you must walk with people who, by their words and their presence, make you wiser. And, to the best of your ability, you must avoid those people who encourage you to think foolish thoughts or do foolish things.

Today, as a gift to yourself, select, from your friends and family members, a mentor whose judgement you trust. Then listen carefully to your mentor's advice and be willing to accept that advice, even if accepting it requires effort, or pain, or both. Consider your mentor to be God's gift to you. Thank God for that gift, and use it.

❧ *If a man knows where to get good advice, it is as though he could supply it himself.*

Goethe

❧ *I have found that the closer I am to the godly people around me, the easier it is for me to live a righteous life because they hold me accountable.*

John MacArthur

❧ *Do you want to be wise? Choose wise friends.*

Charles Swindoll

DAILY DISTRACTIONS

Therefore I say to you, do not worry about your life, what you will eat or what you will drink; nor about your body, what you will put on. Is not life more than food and the body more than clothing?

Matthew 6:25 NKJV

All of us must live through those days when the traffic jams, the computer crashes, and the dog makes a main course out of our homework. But, when we find ourselves distracted by the minor frustrations of life, we must catch ourselves, take a deep breath, and lift our thoughts upward.

Although we may, at times, struggle mightily to rise above the distractions of the everyday living, we need never struggle alone. God is here—eternal and faithful, with infinite patience and love—and, if we reach out to Him, He will restore our sense of perspective and give peace to our souls.

Whatever we focus on determines what we become.

E. Stanley Jones

Jesus did not promise to change the circumstances around us. He promised great peace and pure joy to those who would learn to believe that God actually controls all things.

Corrie ten Boom

A FUTURE SO BRIGHT . . .

*Wisdom is pleasing to you. If you find it,
you have hope for the future.*

Proverbs 24:14 NCV

❧ Are you excited about the opportunities of today *and* thrilled by the possibilities of tomorrow? Do you confidently expect God to lead you to a place of abundance, peace, and joy? And, when your days on earth are over, do you expect to receive the priceless gift of eternal life? If you trust God's promises, and if you have welcomed God's Son into your heart, then you believe that your future is intensely and eternally bright.

Today, as you prepare to meet the duties of everyday life, pause and consider God's promises. And then think for a moment about the wonderful future that awaits *all* believers, including you. God has promised that your future is secure. Trust that promise, and celebrate the life of abundance and eternal joy that is now yours through Christ.

❧ *The Christian believes in a fabulous future.*

Billy Graham

❧ *Take courage. We walk in the wilderness today and in the Promised Land tomorrow.*

D. L. Moody

WHEN GOD SPEAKS QUIETLY

Speak, Lord. I am your servant and I am listening.

1 Samuel 3:10 NCV

❧ Sometimes God speaks loudly and clearly. More often, He speaks in a quiet voice—and if you are wise, you will be listening carefully when He does. To do so, you must carve out quiet moments each day to study His Word and sense His direction.

Can you quiet yourself long enough to listen to your conscience? Are you attuned to the subtle guidance of your intuition? Are you willing to pray sincerely and then to wait quietly for God's response. Hopefully so. Usually God refrains from sending His messages on stone tablets or city billboards. More often, He communicates in subtler ways. If you sincerely desire to hear His voice, you must listen carefully, and you must do so in the silent corners of your quiet, willing heart.

❧ *Most of man's trouble comes from his inability to be still.*

Blaise Pascal

❧ *Noise and words and frenzied, hectic schedules dull our senses, closing our ears to His still, small voice and making us numb to His touch.*

Charles Swindoll

RIGHTEOUSNESS AND RIGHTNESS

Christ ended the law so that everyone who believes in him may be right with God.

Romans 10:4 NCV

❧ How do we live a life that is "right with God"? By accepting God's Son and obeying His commandments. Accepting Christ is a decision that we make one time; following in His footsteps requires thousands of decisions each day.

Whose steps will you follow today? Will you honor God as you strive to follow His Son? Or will you join the lockstep legion that seeks to discover happiness and fulfillment through worldly means? If you are righteous and wise, you will follow Christ. You will follow Him today and every day. You will seek to walk in His footsteps without reservation or doubt. When you do so, you will be "right with God" precisely because you are walking aright with His only begotten Son.

❧ *It is the highest duty of religion to imitate Him whom you adore.*

St. Augustine of Hippo

❧ *For nourishment, comfort, exhilaration, and refreshment, no wine can rival the love of Jesus. Drink deeply.*

C. H. Spurgeon

HOPE NOW!

Hope deferred makes the heart sick.

Proverbs 13:12 NKJV

❦ The hope that the world offers is fleeting and imperfect. The hope that God offers is unchanging, unshakable, and unending. It is no wonder, then, that when we seek security from worldly sources, our are hopes are often dashed. Thankfully, God has no such record of failure.

Where will you place your hopes today? Will you entrust your future to man or to God? Will you seek solace exclusively from fallible human beings, or will you place your hopes, first and foremost, in the trusting hands of your Creator? The decision is yours, and you must live with the results of the choice you make.

For thoughtful believers, hope begins with God. Period. So today, as you embark upon the next stage of your life's journey, consider the words of the Psalmist: "You are my hope, O Lord God; You are my trust from my youth" (71:5 NKJV). Then, place your trust in the One who cannot be shaken.

❦ *The choice for me is to either look at all things I have lost or the things I have. To live in fear or to live in hope…. Hope comes from knowing I have a sovereign, loving God who is in every event in my life.*

Lisa Beamer
(Her husband Todd was killed on flight 93, 9-11-01)

WHERE THE SPIRIT LEADS

*The true children of God are those
who let God's Spirit lead them.*

Romans 8:14 NCV

❧ Paul encourages believers to filled with the Spirit of God: "Do not be drunk with wine, which will ruin you, but be filled with the Spirit" (Ephesians 5:18 NCV). When you are filled with the Holy Spirit, you words and deeds will reflect a love and devotion to Christ. When you are filled with the Holy Sprit, the steps of your life's journey are guided by the Lord. When you allow God's Spirit to work in you and through you, you will be energized and transformed.

Today, allow yourself to be filled with the Spirit of God. And then stand back in amazement as God begins to work miracles in your own life *and* in the lives of those you love.

❧ *I feel my weakness and inability to accomplish anything without the aid of the Holy Spirit.*

Lottie Moon

❧ *Whether we preach, pray, write, do business, travel, take care of children, or administer the government— whatever we do—our whole life and influence should be filled with the power of the Holy Spirit.*

Charles Finney

BEING TRUE TO YOURSELF . . . AND TO GOD

The righteous man walks in his integrity;
his children are blessed after him.

Proverbs 20:7 NKJV

❧ When God made you, He equipped you with an array of talents and abilities that are uniquely yours. It's up to you to discover those talents and to use them, but sometimes the world will encourage you to do otherwise. At times, our society will attempt to cubbyhole you, to standardize you, and to make you fit into particular, preformed mold. God has other plans.

Have you found something in this life that you're passionate about? Something that inspires you to jump out of bed in the morning and hit the ground running? And does your work honor the Creator by making His world a better place? If so, congratulations: You're using your gifts well.

Sometimes, because you're a fallible human being, you may become so wrapped up in meeting *society's* expectations that you fail to focus on *God's* expectations. To do so is a mistake of major proportions—don't make it.

What's the best way to thank God for the gifts that He has given you? By using them. Today.

❧ *Maintaining your integrity in a world of sham is no small accomplishment.*

Wayne Oates

The Futility of Foolish Arguments

But stay away from those who have foolish arguments
and talk about useless family histories and argue
and quarrel about the law. Those things are
worth nothing and will not help anyone.

Titus 3:9 NCV

❧ Arguments are seldom won but often lost. When we engage in petty squabbles, our losses usually outpace our gains. When we acquire the unfortunate habit of habitual bickering, we do harm to our friends, to our families, to our coworkers, and to ourselves.

Time and again, God's Word warns us that most arguments are a monumental waste of time, of energy, of life. In Titus, we are warned to refrain from "foolish arguments," and with good reason. Such arguments usually do more for the devil than they do for God.

So the next time you're tempted to engage in a silly squabble, whether inside the church or outside it, refrain. When you do, you'll put a smile on God's face, and you'll send the devil packing.

❧ *I have noticed in study and in experience that the more vital and important any theological or doctrinal truth may be, the devil will fight it harder and bring greater controversy to bear upon it.*

A. W. Tozer

DUTY TO GOD AND MANKIND

Well done, good and faithful servant; you were faithful over a few things, I will make you ruler over many things. Enter into the joy of your lord.

Matthew 25:21 NKJV

❦ God has promised us this: When we do our duties in small matters, He will give us additional responsibilities. When we do our work dutifully, and when we behave responsibly, God rewards us—in a time and in a manner of His choosing, not our own.

Sometimes, God rewards us by giving us additional burdens to bear, or by changing the course of our lives so that we may better serve Him. Sometimes, our rewards come in the form of temporary setbacks that lead, in turn, to greater victories. Sometimes, God rewards us by answering "no" to our prayers so that He can say "yes" to a far grander request that we, with our limited understanding, would never have thought to ask for.

If you seek to be God's servant in great matters, be faithful, be patient, and be dutiful in smaller matters. Then step back and watch as God surprises you with the spectacular creativity of His infinite wisdom and His perfect plan.

❦ *When the law of God is written on our hearts, our duty will be our delight.*

Matthew Henry

A THIRST FOR GOD

My soul thirsts for God, for the living God.
Psalms 42:2 NKJV

❧ Where is God? He is everywhere you have ever been and everywhere you will ever go. He is with you throughout the night and all through the day; He knows your every thought; He hears your every heartbeat.

When you earnestly seek Him, you will find Him because He is here, waiting patiently for you to reach out to Him . . . right here . . . right now. And make no mistake: Your soul does indeed thirst for God. That thirst that is planted in you heart, and it is a thirst that only God can quench. Let Him. . . right here . . . right now.

❧ _To a world that was spiritually dry and populated with parched lives scorched by sin, Jesus was the Living Water who would quench the thirsty soul._

Anne Graham Lotz

❧ _Our souls were made to live in an upper atmosphere, and we stifle and choke if we live on any lower level. Our eyes were made to look off from these heavenly heights, and our vision is distorted by any lower gazing._

Hannah Whitall Smith

Wed

THE LIFE TO WHICH YOU ARE CALLED

*So I urge you now to live the life to which
God called you.*

Ephesians 4:1 NCV

❧ "What does God intend for me to do with the rest of my life?" It's an easy question to ask, but, for many of us, a difficult question to answer. Why? Because God's purposes aren't always clear to us. Sometimes we wander aimlessly in a spiritual desert of our own design. And sometimes, we struggle mightily against God in a vain effort to find success and happiness through the world's means, not His.

How can we know *precisely* what God's plan are for our lives? The answer, of course, that we cannot know *precisely* what God intends; what we can do is this: We can study His Word, we can pray for His guidance, we can obey His commandments; and we can trust His direction. And that is *precisely* what we should do.

❧ *God custom-designed you with your unique combination of personality, temperament, talents, and background, and He wants to harness and use these in His mission to reach this messed-up world.*

Bill Hybels

❧ *The place where God calls you is the place where your deep gladness and the world's deep hunger meet.*

Frederick Buechner

LIVING SIMPLY IN
A COMPLICATED WORLD

And do not be conformed to this world,
but be transformed by the renewing of your mind..
Romans 12:2 NKJV

❧ Is yours a life of moderation or accumulation? Are you more interested in the possessions you can acquire or in the person you can become? The answers to these questions will determine the direction of your day and, in time, the direction of your life.

Ours is a highly complicated society, a place where people and corporations vie for your attention, for your time, and for your dollars. Don't let them succeed in complicating your life! Keep your eyes focused instead upon God.

If your material possessions are somehow distancing you from God, discard them. If your outside interests leave you too little time for your family or your God, slow down the merry-go-round, or better yet, get off completely. Remember: God wants your full attention, and He wants it today, so don't let anybody or anything get in His way.

❧ *We Christians must simplify our lives or lose untold treasures on earth and in eternity. Modern civilization is so complex as to make the devotional life all but impossible. The need for solitude and quietness was never greater than it is today.*
A. W. Tozer

CHEERFUL CHRISTIANITY

The cheerful heart has a continual feast.

Proverbs 15:15 NIV

🌿 Few things in life are more sad, or, for that matter, more absurd, than a grumpy Christian. Christ promises us lives of abundance and joy, but He does not force His joy upon us. We must claim His joy for ourselves, and when we do, Jesus, in turn, fills our spirits with His power and His love.

How can we receive from Christ the joy that is rightfully ours? By giving Him what is rightfully His: our hearts and our souls. When we earnestly commit ourselves to the Savior of mankind, when we place Jesus at the center of our lives and trust Him as our *personal* Savior, He transforms us, not just for today, but for all eternity. Then, we, as God's children, can share Christ's joy and His message with a world that desperately needs both.

🌿 *When I think of God, my heart is full of joy. Since God has given me a cheerful heart, I serve him with a cheerful spirit.*

Franz Joseph Haydn

🌿 *The people whom I have seen succeed best in life have always been cheerful and hopeful people who went about their business with a smile on their faces.*

Charles Kingsley

REMEMBERING GOD'S LOVE

For the Lord is good; His mercy is everlasting,
and His truth endures to all generations.

Psalms 100:5 NKJV

❧ The Bible tells us that God is love and that if we wish to know Him, we must have love in our hearts. Yet there are times, especially when we're tired, angry, or frustrated, that it is hard for us to be loving. Thankfully, anger and frustration are feelings that come and go, but God's love endures forever.

Today, as a gift to yourself and your loved ones, make time to express the love that you feel in your heart. Share the love that God has placed there. His love never fails; His love never falters. His love, unlike our own, is perfect. And His love must be spread throughout the world—beginning now, beginning here, beginning with you.

❧ *Love, for instance, is not something God has which may grow or diminish or cease to be. His love is the way God is, and when He loves He is simply being Himself.*

A. W. Tozer

❧ *We are the mirrors of God's love, so we may show Jesus by our lives.*

Corrie ten Boom

THE IMPORTANCE OF WORDS

*So then, rid yourselves of all evil, all lying, hypocrisy,
jealousy, and evil speech. As newborn babies want
milk, you should want the pure and simple teaching.
By it you can grow up and be saved.*

1 Peter 2:1, 2 NCV

❧ How important are the words we speak? More important than we realize. Our words have echoes that extend beyond place or time. If our words are encouraging, we can lift others up; if our words are hurtful, we can hold others back.

Do you seek to be a source of encouragement to others? And, do you seek to be a worthy ambassador for Christ? If so, you must speak words that are worthy of your Savior. So avoid angry outbursts. Refrain from impulsive outpourings. Terminate tantrums. Instead, speak words of encouragement and hope to your family and friends, who, by the way, most certainly need all the hope and encouragement they can find.

❧ *Words. Do you fully understand their power? Can any of us really grasp the mighty force behind the things we say? Do we stop and think before we speak, considering the potency of the words we utter?*

Joni Eareckson Tada

❧ *The great test of a man's character is his tongue.*

Oswald Chambers

MAKING THE MOST OF WHATEVER COMES

A man's heart plans his way,
but the Lord directs his steps.

Proverbs 16:9 NKJV

🌿 God's hand shapes the world, and it shapes your life. So wherever you find yourself—whether on the mountaintop or in the darkest valley—remember that God is there, too. And He's ready to help.

Are you willing to accept God's help by prayerfully opening your heart to Him? And are you willing to conform your will to His? If so, then you can be certain that you and God, working together, will make the most of whatever comes your way.

🌿 *A wise man turns chance into good fortune.*

Thomas Fuller

🌿 *The most profane word we use is "hopeless." When you say a situation or person is hopeless, you are slamming the door in the face of God.*

Kathy Troccoli

🌿 *Great opportunities often disguise themselves in small tasks.*

Rick Warren

true

OUR ACTIONS REVEAL OUR BELIEFS

Therefore by their fruits you will know them.

Matthew 7:20 NKJV

❧ English clergyman Thomas Fuller observed, "He does not believe who does not live according to his beliefs." These words are most certainly true. We may proclaim our beliefs to our hearts' content, but our proclamations will mean nothing—to others *or* to ourselves—unless we accompany our words with deeds that match. The sermons that we live are far more compelling than the ones we preach.

Like it or not, your life is an accurate reflection of your creed. If this fact gives you some cause for concern, don't bother *talking* about the changes that you intend to make—make them. And then, when your good deeds speak for themselves—as they most certainly will—*don't* interrupt.

❧ *What you do reveals what you believe about God, regardless of what you say. When God reveals what He has purposed to do, you face a crisis—a decision time. God and the world can tell from your response what you really believe about God.*

Henry Blackaby

❧ *What we believe determines how we behave, and both determine what we become.*

Warren Wiersbe

Wed

ACCEPTANCE FOR TODAY

To You, O my Strength, I will sing praises;
for God is my defense, my God of mercy.
Psalm 59:17 NKJV

❧ Manmade plans are fallible; God's plans are not. Yet whenever life takes an unexpected turn, we are tempted to fall into the spiritual traps of worry, self-pity, or bitterness. God intends that we do otherwise.

The old saying is familiar: "Forgive and forget." But when we have been hurt badly, forgiveness is often difficult and forgetting is downright impossible. Since we can't forget yesterday's troubles, we should learn from them. Yesterday has much to teach us about tomorrow. We may *learn* from the past, but we should never *live* in the past. God has given each of us a glorious day: this one. And it's up to each of us to use this day as faithful stewards, not as embittered historians.

So if you're trying to forget the past, don't waste your time. Instead, try a different approach: Learn to *accept* the past and *live* in the present. Then, you can focus your thoughts and your energies, not on the struggles of yesterday, but instead on the profound opportunities that God has placed before you *today*.

❧ *Fretting springs from a determination to get our own way.*
Oswald Chambers

STUDYING GOD'S WORD

As newborn babies want milk,
you should want the pure and simple teaching.
By it you can grow up and be saved.

1 Peter 2:2 NCV

❧ As a spiritual being, you have the potential to grow in your personal knowledge of the Lord every day that you live. You can do so through prayer, through worship, through an openness to God's Holy Spirits, and through a careful study of God's Holy Word.

Your Bible contains powerful prescriptions for everyday living. If you sincerely seek to walk with God, you should commit yourself to the thoughtful study of His teachings. The Bible can and should be your roadmap for every aspect of your life.

Do you seek to establish a closer relationship with your Heavenly Father? Then study His Word every day, with no exceptions. The Holy Bible is a priceless, one-of-a-kind gift from God. Treat it that way *and* read it that way.

❧ *Be filled with the Holy Spirit; join a church where the members believe the Bible and know the Lord; seek the fellowship of other Christians; learn and be nourished by God's Word and His many promises. Conversion is not the end of your journey—it is only the beginning.*

Corrie ten Boom

DISOBEDIENCE EQUALS DISASTER

You shall walk after the Lord your God and fear Him,
and keep His commandments and obey His voice,
and you shall serve Him and hold fast to Him.

Deuteronomy 13:4 NKJV

❧ As creatures of free will, we may disobey God whenever we choose, but when we do so, we put ourselves and our loved ones in peril. Why? Because disobedience invites disaster. We cannot sin against God without consequence. We cannot live outside His will without injury. We cannot distance ourselves from God without hardening our hearts. We cannot yield to the ever-tempting distractions of our world and, at the same time, enjoy God's peace.

Sometimes, in a futile attempt to justify our behaviors, we make a distinction between "big" sins and "little" ones. To do so is a mistake of "big" proportions. Sins of all shapes and sizes have the power to do us great harm. And in a world where sin is big business, that's certainly a sobering thought.

❧ *Sin for a man is a disorder and perversion: that is, a turning away from the most worthy Creator and a turning toward the inferior things that He has created.*

St. Augustine of Hippo

GOD'S GOLDEN RULE

Therefore, whatever you want men to do to you,
do also to them, for this is the Law and the Prophets.

Matthew 7:12 NKJV

❧ The words of Matthew 7:12 remind us that, as believers in Christ, we are commanded to treat others as we wish to be treated. This commandment is, indeed, the Golden Rule for Christians of every generation. When we weave the thread of kindness into the very fabric of our lives, we give glory to the One who gave His life for ours.

Because we are imperfect human beings, we are, on occasion, selfish, thoughtless, or cruel. But God commands us to behave otherwise. He teaches us to rise above our own imperfections and to treat others with unselfishness and love. When we observe God's Golden Rule, we help build His kingdom here on earth. And, when we share the love of Christ, we share a priceless gift; may we share it today and every day that we live.

❧ *One of the greatest things a man can do for his heavenly Father is to be kind to some of his other children.*

Henry Drummond

❧ *It's not difficult to make an impact on your world. All you really have to do is put the needs of others ahead of your own. You can make a difference with a little time and a big heart.*

James Dobson

TRUST IN A LOVING FATHER

If God is for us, who can be against us?

Romans 8:31 NKJV

❧ What do you expect from the day ahead? Are you expecting God to do wonderful things, or are you living beneath a cloud of apprehension and doubt? The familiar words of Psalm 118:24 remind us of a profound yet simple truth: "This is the day the Lord has made; we will rejoice and be glad in it" (NKJV).

For Christian believers, every day begins and ends with God's Son and God's promises. When we accept Christ into our hearts, God promises us the opportunity for earthy peace and spiritual abundance. But more importantly, God promises us the priceless gift of eternal life.

As we face the inevitable challenges of life here on earth, we must arm ourselves with the promises of God's Holy Word. When we do, we can expect the best, not only for the day ahead, but also for every day thereafter.

❧ *You have loved us first; help us never to forget that You are love so that this sure conviction might triumph in our hearts over the seduction of the world, over the inquietude of the soul, over the anxiety for the future, over the fright of the past, over the distress of the moment.*

Søren Kierkegaard

THE RIGHT KIND OF WISDOM

Only the Lord gives wisdom;
he gives knowledge and understanding.

Proverbs 2:6 NCV

❧ Sometimes, amid the concerns of everyday life, we lose perspective. Life seems out of balance, and the pressures may seem overwhelming. What's needed is a renewed faith, a fresh perspective, and God's wisdom.

Here in the 21ˢᵗ century, commentary is commonplace, information is, for practical purposes, infinite, and education is available almost everywhere. But the ultimate source of wisdom, the kind of timeless wisdom that God willingly shares with His children, is still available from a single unique source: the Holy Bible.

The wisdom of the world changes with the ever-shifting sands of public opinion. God's wisdom does not. His wisdom is eternal. It never changes. And it most certainly is the wisdom that you must use to plan your day, your life, and your eternal destiny.

❧ _The person who is wise spiritually, who is a true Christian, builds his life and performs his duties carefully, realizing the great substance and importance involved._

John MacArthur

OFFERING COMFORT TO THOSE IN NEED

*Now we exhort you, brethren, warn those
who are unruly, comfort the fainthearted,
uphold the weak, be patient with all.*

1 Thessalonians 5:14 NKJV

The 118th Psalm reminds us, "This is the day which the Lord hath made; we will rejoice and be glad in it" (v. 24 KJV). As we rejoice in this day that the Lord has given us, let us remember that an important part of today's celebration is the time we spend comforting those in need.

Each day provides countless opportunities to encourage others and to assist those who cannot assist themselves. When we do, we not only spread seeds of hope and happiness, we also follow the commandments of God's Holy Word.

Today, someone very near you needs a helping hand or a comforting word. Be generous with both, just as your Heavenly Father has been generous with you.

So often we think that to be encouragers we have to produce great words of wisdom when, in fact, a few simple syllables of sympathy and an arm around the shoulder can often provide much needed comfort.

Florence Littauer

Wed

LOVING AND OBEYING GOD

*For this is the love of God, that we keep
His commandments. And His commandments
are not burdensome.*

1 John 2:5, 6 NKJV

❧ C. S. Lewis observed, "A man's spiritual health is exactly proportional to his love for God." If we are to enjoy the spiritual health that God intends for our lives, we must praise Him, we must love Him, and we must obey Him.

When we worship God faithfully and obediently, when we place Him at the absolute center of our lives, we invite His love into our hearts. In turn, we grow to love God more deeply as we sense His love for us. St. Augustine wrote, "I love you, Lord, not doubtingly, but with absolute certainty. Your Word beat upon my heart until I fell in love with you, and now the universe and everything in it tells me to love you."

Let us pray that we, too, will open our hearts to our Father. And let our obedience be a response to His never-ending love.

❧ *It is the Lord Jesus Christ who stands as the focus of our obedience. Our union with Him—the One Who spoke words of life and finished a redemptive work—is that out of which our obedience flows.*

Helmut Thielicke

PLANNING AND DILIGENCE

The plans of hard-working people earn a profit,
but those who act too quickly become poor.

Proverbs 21:5 NCV

❧ Are you willing to plan for the future—and are you willing to work diligently to accomplish the plans that you've made? The Book of Proverbs teaches that the plans of hardworking people (like you) are rewarded.

If you desire to reap a bountiful harvest from life, you must plan for the future while entrusting the final outcome to God. Then, you must do your part to make the future better (by working diligently), while acknowledging the sovereignty of God's hands over all affairs, including your own.

Are you in a hurry for success to arrive at your doorstep? Don't be. Instead, work diligently, plan carefully, and wait patiently. And remember that you're not the only one working on your behalf; God is at work, too. And with Him as your partner, your success is guaranteed.

❧ *It may be that the day of judgment will dawn tomorrow; in that case, we shall gladly stop working for a better tomorrow. But not before.*

Dietrich Bonhoeffer

❧ *Success and happiness are not destinations. They are exciting, never-ending journeys.*

Zig Ziglar

THE POWER OF PATIENCE

Patience is better than strength.
Controlling your temper is better than
capturing a city.

Proverbs 16:32 NCV

❧ Temper tantrums are usually unproductive, un-attractive, unforgettable, and unnecessary. Perhaps that's why Proverbs 16:32 states that, "Controlling your temper is better than capturing a city."

If you've allowed anger to become a regular visitor at your house, today you must pray for wisdom, for patience, and for a heart that is so filled with love and forgiveness that it contains no room for bitterness. God will help you terminate your tantrums *if* you ask Him to. And God can help you to perfect your ability to be patient *if* you ask Him to. So ask Him, and then wait patiently for the ever-more-patient you to arrive.

❧ *As long as anger lives, she continues to be the fruitful mother of many unhappy children.*

John Climacus

❧ *When I am dealing with an all-powerful, all-knowing God, I, as a mere mortal, must offer my petitions not only with persistence, but also with patience. Someday I'll know why.*

Ruth Bell Graham

UNRELIABLE THINKING

Do not worry about anything, but pray and ask God for everything you need, always giving thanks.

Philippians 4:6 NCV

❧ Charles Swindoll advises, "When you're on the verge of throwing a pity party thanks to your despairing thoughts, go back to the Word of God." How true. Self-pity is not only an unproductive way to think, it is also an affront to God.

God's Word promises that believers can receive abundance, peace, love, and eternal life. These gifts are not earned; they are an outpouring from God, a manifestation of His grace. Self-pity and peace cannot coexist in the same mind. Bitterness and joy cannot coexist in the same heart. Thanksgiving and despair are mutually exclusive.

If your unreliable thoughts are allowing pain and worry to dominate your life, you must train yourself to think less about your troubles and more about God's blessings. And when you stop to think about it, hasn't He given you enough blessings to occupy your thoughts all day, every day, from now on? Of course He has! So focus your thoughts on God's blessings, and let your worries fend for themselves.

❧ *Worry is a cycle of inefficient thoughts whirling around a center of fear.*

Corrie ten Boom

WORDS SPEAK LOUDER

In every way be an example of doing good deeds.
When you teach, do it with honesty and seriousness.

Titus 2:7 NCV

❧ Our words speak, but our actions speak far more loudly. Whether we like it or not, all of us are role models. Our friends and family members watch our actions and, as followers of Christ, we are obliged to act accordingly.

Corrie ten Boom advised, "Don't worry about what you do not understand. Worry about what you do understand in the Bible but do not live by." And that's sound advice because our families and friends are watching . . . and so, for that matter, is God.

❧ *Actions speak louder than words; let your words teach and your actions speak.*

Anthony of Padua

❧ *For one man who can introduce another to Jesus Christ by the way he lives and by the atmosphere of his life, there are a thousand who can only talk jargon about him.*

Oswald Chambers

LIVING WITH THE LIVING WORD

He who heeds the word wisely will find good,
and whoever trusts in the Lord, happy is he.

Proverbs 16:20 NKJV

❧ Are you sincerely seeking to discover God's will and follow it? If so, study His Word and obey His commandments. The words of Matthew 4:4 remind us that, "Man shall not live by bread alone, but by every word that proceeds from the mouth of God." (NKJV). As believers, we must study the Bible and meditate upon its meaning for our lives. Otherwise, we deprive ourselves of a priceless gift from our Creator.

Jonathan Edwards advised, "Be assiduous in reading the Holy Scriptures. This is the fountain whence all knowledge in divinity must be derived. Therefore let not this treasure lie by you neglected." God's Holy Word is, indeed, a priceless, one-of-a-kind treasure, and a passing acquaintance with the Good Book is insufficient for Christians who seek to obey God's Word and to understand His will. After all, man does not live by bread alone . . .

❧ *God has given us all sorts of counsel and direction in his written Word; thank God, we have it written down in black and white.*

John Eldredge

FINDING THE NEW AND BETTER WAY

*When we were baptized, we were buried with Christ
and shared his death. So, just as Christ was raised
from the dead by the wonderful power of the Father,
we also can live a new life.*

Romans 6:4 NCV

❧ For Christian believers, every day begins and ends with God and with His only begotten Son. Christ came to this earth to give us abundant life and eternal salvation. Our task is to accept Christ's grace with joy in our hearts and praise on our lips. Believers who fashion their days around Jesus are transformed: They see the world differently, they act differently, and they feel differently about themselves and their neighbors.

Christian believers face the inevitable challenges and disappointments of each day armed with the joy of Christ and the promise of salvation. So whatever this day holds for you, begin it and end it with God as your partner and Christ as your Savior. And throughout the day, give thanks to the One who created you and saved you. God's love for you is infinite. Accept it joyously and be thankful.

❧ *The essence of salvation is an about-face from self-centeredness to God-centeredness.*

Henry Blackaby

GROWING WITH AND BEYOND OUR TROUBLES

We also have joy with our troubles, because we know that these troubles produce patience. And patience produces character, and character produces hope.

Romans 5:3, 4 NCV

❦ The times that try your soul are also the times that build your character. During the darker days of life, you can learn lessons that are impossible to learn during sunny, happier days. Times of adversity can—and should—be times of intense spiritual and personal growth. But God will not force you to learn the lessons of adversity. You must learn them for yourself.

The next time Old Man Trouble knocks on your door, remember that he has lessons to teach. So turn him away quickly as you can, but learn his lessons while you're doing so. And remember: The trouble with trouble isn't just the trouble it causes; it's also the trouble we cause *ourselves* if we ignore the things that trouble has to teach us.

❦ *Character cannot be developed in ease and quiet. Only through experience of trial and suffering can the soul be strengthened, vision cleared, ambition inspired, and success achieved.*

Helen Keller

LOVING ENOUGH TO OVERLOOK

*And above all things have fervent love for one another,
for "love will cover a multitude of sins."*

1 Peter 4:8 NKJV

❧ Genuine love is an exercise in forgiveness. If we wish to build lasting relationships, we must learn how to forgive. Why? Because our loved ones are imperfect (as are we). How often must we forgive our family and friends? More times than we can count; to do otherwise is to disobey God.

Perhaps granting forgiveness is hard for you. If so, you are not alone. Genuine, lasting forgiveness is often difficult to achieve—difficult but not impossible. Thankfully, with God's help, all things are possible, and that includes forgiveness. But even though God is willing to help, He expects you to do some of the work. And make no mistake: Forgiveness is work, which is okay with God. He knows that the payoffs are worth the effort.

❧ *Forgiveness is the final form of love.*

Reinhold Niebuhr

❧ *Love is not soft as water is; it is solid as a rock on which the waves of hatred beat in vain.*

Corrie ten Boom

OBEDIENCE AND SERVICE

If anyone serves Me, let him follow Me;
and where I am, there My servant will be also.
If anyone serves Me, him My Father will honor.

John 12:26 NKJV

❧ As you seek to discover God's purpose for your life, you may rest assured that His plan for you is centered around service to your family, to your friends, to your church, to your community, and to the world. God intends that you work diligently on His behalf to serve His children and to share His Good News.

Whom will you choose to serve today? The needs are great and the workers are few. And God is doing His very best to enlist able-bodied believers—like you.

❧ *Following Jesus means living as obedient servants of his heavenly Father and ministering—even suffering—for the sake of others.*

Stanley Grenz

❧ *Make this day a day of obedience, a day of spiritual joy, and a day of peace. Make this day's work a little part of the work of the Kingdom of my Lord Christ.*

John Baillie

❧ *There is nothing small in the service of God.*

Francis of Sales

The Power of Christian Fellowship

*Behold, how good and how pleasant it is for brethren
to dwell together in unity!*

Psalm 133:1 NKJV

It is almost impossible to underestimate the importance of Christian fellowship. When you join with fellow believers in worship and praise, you enrich their lives in the same way they enrich yours.

Christ promised that wherever two or more are gathered together in His name, He is there also (Matthew 18:20). So let us gather together in the presence of Christ and worship Him with thanksgiving in our hearts, praise on our lips, and fellow believers by our sides.

A vibrant fellowship of believers is one of our greatest apologetics for the truth of the gospel.

Stanley Grenz

Christians are like the flowers in a garden: they have upon them the dew of heaven, which, being shaken by the wind, they let fall at each other's roots, whereby they are jointly nourished.

John Bunyan

Blest be the tie that binds our hearts in Christian love; the fellowship of kindred minds is like to that above.

John Fawcett

Part of God's Family

*For whoever does the will of God is My brother
and My sister and mother.*

Mark 3:35 NKJV

₮ As human beings with limited understanding, we can never fully understand the will of God. But as believers in a benevolent God, we must always trust the will of our Heavenly Father. When we do so, we become part of God's family.

As this day unfolds, seek God's will for your own life and obey His Word. When you entrust your life to Him completely and without reservation, He will give you the strength to meet any challenge, the courage to face any trial, and the wisdom to live in His righteousness and in His peace.

₮ *If my life is surrendered to God, all is well. Let me not grab it back, as though it were in peril in His hand but would be safer in mine!*

Elisabeth Elliot

₮ *The center of power is not to be found in summit meetings or in peace conferences. It is not in Peking or Washington or the United Nations, but rather where a child of God prays in the power of the Spirit for God's will to be done in her life, in her home, and in the world around her.*

Ruth Bell Graham

OUR INTENTIONS ARE
IMPORTANT TO GOD

Every way of a man is right in his own eyes,
but the Lord weighs the hearts.

Proverbs 21:2 NKJV

Ꮕ The world sees you as you appear to be; God sees you as you really are . . . He sees your heart and He understands your intentions.

The opinions that others may have of you are relatively unimportant; God's view of you, however, is vitally important. Your challenge, of course, is to concern yourself with God's opinion of your thoughts, your motivations, and your actions. Few things in life are more futile than "keeping up appearances" for the sake of our neighbors. What *is* important, of course, is pleasing our Father in heaven. We do so when our intentions are pure and our actions are just.

Ꮕ *Let us learn to cast our hearts into God.*

Bernard of Clairvaux

Ꮕ *There is no other method of living piously and justly than that of depending upon God.*

John Calvin

Ꮕ *The more wisdom enters our hearts, the more we will be able to trust our hearts in difficult situations.*

John Eldredge

COURAGE FOR TODAY . . .
AND FOREVER

Don't be afraid, because I am your God.
I will make you strong and will help you;
I will support you with my right hand that saves you.

Isaiah 41:10 NCV

☙ Christians have every reason to live courageously. After all, the ultimate battle has already been won on the cross at Calvary. But even dedicated followers of Christ may find their courage tested by the inevitable disappointments and fears that visit the lives of believers and non-believers alike.

When you find yourself worried about the challenges of today or the uncertainties of tomorrow, you must ask yourself whether or not you are ready to place your concerns and your life in God's all-powerful, all-knowing, all-loving hands.

☙ *I pray that God will convince you of your security in Christ. I pray that he will remind you that your name is engraved on his hands. I pray that you will hear him whisper, "So do not fear, for I am with you" (Isaiah 41:10).*

C. H. Spurgeon

☙ *If a person fears God, he or she has no reason to fear anything else. On the other hand, if a person does not fear God, then fear becomes a way of life.*

Beth Moore

STRENGTH FOR TOUGH TIMES

*If you faint in the day of adversity,
your strength is small.*

Proverbs 24:10 NKJV

From time to time, all of us face adversity, hardship, disappointment, and loss. Old Man Trouble pays periodic visits to each of us; none of us are exempt. When we are troubled, God stands ready and willing to protect us. Our responsibility, of course, is to ask Him for protection. When we call upon Him in heartfelt prayer, He will answer—in His own time and in accordance with His own perfect plan.

Our world continues to change, but God's love remains constant. And, He remains ready to comfort us and strengthen us whenever we turn to Him. Psalm 145 promises, "The Lord is near to all who call upon Him, To all who call upon Him in truth. He will fulfill the desire of those who fear Him; He also will hear their cry and save them." (v. 18, 19 NKJV).

Life is often challenging, but as Christians, we must not be afraid. God loves us, and He will protect us. In times of hardship, He will comfort us; in times of sorrow, He will dry our tears. When we are troubled, or weak, or sorrowful, God is always with us. We must build our lives on the rock that cannot be shaken…we must trust in God. Always.

As sure as God puts his children in the furnace, he will be in the furnace with them.

C. H. Spurgeon

EXPECTING GREAT THINGS

When a believing person prays, great things happen.
James 5:16 NCV

ⅎ James 5:16 makes the promise that God intends to keep: When you pray earnestly, fervently, and often, great things will happen. Too many of us, however, are too timid or too pessimistic to ask God to do big things. So we pray, not with a sense of expectation, but with a sense of reservation.

God can and will do great things through you if you have the courage to ask Him and the determination to keep asking Him. Honor Him by making big requests. But don't expect Him to do all the work. When you do your part, He will do His part. And when He does, expect a miracle . . . a _big_ miracle.

ⅎ _We honor God by asking for great things when they are a part of His promise. We dishonor Him and cheat ourselves when we ask for molehills where He has promised mountains._

Vance Havner

ⅎ _When you affirm big, believe big, and pray big, big things happen._

Norman Vincent Peale

THE DANGERS OF PRIDE

Pride leads only to shame; it is wise to be humble.

Proverbs 11:2 NCV

☞ The words from Proverbs 11 remind us that pride and destruction are traveling partners. But as imperfect human beings, we are tempted to puff our chests and crow about our own accomplishments. When we do so, we delude ourselves.

As Christians, we have a profound reason to be humble: We have been refashioned and saved by Jesus Christ, and that salvation came not because of our own good works but because of God's grace. Thus, we are not "self-made," we are "God-made," and "Christ-saved." How, then, can we be boastful? The answer, of course, is simple: If we are honest with ourselves and with our God, we cannot be boastful. In the quiet moments, when we search the depths of our own hearts, we know that whatever "it" is, God did *that*. And He deserves the credit.

☞ *The Lord sends no one away empty except those who are full of themselves.*

D. L. Moody

☞ *The reason why God is so great a Lover of humility is because He is the great Lover of truth. Now humility is nothing but truth, while pride is nothing but lying.*

St. Vincent de Paul

THE JOY OF SERVING OUR HEAVENLY FATHER

Enjoy serving the Lord,
and he will give you what you want.

Psalm 37:4 NCV

🎵 Are you excited about serving God? You should be. As a believer living in today's challenging world, you have countless opportunities to honor your Father in Heaven by serving Him.

Far too many Christians seem bored with their faith and stressed by their service. Don't allow your self to become one of them! Serve God with thanksgiving in your heart and praise on your lips. Make your service to Him a time of celebration and thanksgiving. Worship your Creator by *working* for Him, joyfully, faithfully, *and* often.

🎵 *God wants us to serve Him with a willing spirit, one that would choose no other way.*

Beth Moore

🎵 *Holy service in constant fellowship with God is heaven below.*

C. H. Spurgeon

WALKING WITH THE WORD, WALKING IN THE LIGHT

Your word is a lamp to my feet and a light to my path.
Psalm 119:105 NKJV

⁂ Is God's Word a lamp that guides your path? Is God's Word your indispensable compass for everyday living, or is it relegated to Sunday morning services? Do you read the Bible faithfully or sporadically? The answer to these questions will determine the direction of your thoughts, the direction of your day, and the direction of your life.

God's Word can be a roadmap to a place of righteous and abundance. Make it _your_ roadmap. God's wisdom can be a light to guide your steps. Claim it as _your_ light today, tomorrow, and every day of your life—and then walk confidently in the footsteps of God's only begotten Son.

⁂ _Has he taken over your heart? Perhaps he resides there, but does he preside there?_
Vance Havner

⁂ _Love Holy Scripture, and wisdom will love you. Love Scripture, and she will keep you. Honor her, and she will keep you._
St. Augustine

⁂ _Faith does not concern itself with the entire journey. One step is enough._
Mrs. Charles E. Cowman

PLANTING THE SEEDS OF FAITH

Let us hold fast the confession of our hope without wavering, for He who promised is faithful.

Hebrews 10:23 NKJV

ℬ Life, like a garden, is a leap of faith. We plant our seeds in God's good earth, and we expect Him to bring forth a plentiful harvest. And so it is when we plant the seeds of faith in our hearts: When we trust God completely, He brings forth a bountiful harvest in our lives, a harvest of abundance, joy, and peace.

Jesus Christ is the ultimate savior of humanity and the personal Savior of those who believe in Him. As his servants, we must place Him at the very center of our lives, not on the periphery. When we form a personal bond with our Savior, the seeds of our faith will multiply and flourish not only for today, but also for eternity.

ℬ *Christ is the principle object about which faith is exercised, for the obtaining of righteousness and everlasting happiness.*

Thomas Brooks

ℬ *Faith is greater than learning.*

Martin Luther

SHINING LIKE STARS

*The wise people will shine like the brightness of
the sky. Those who teach others to live right
will shine like stars forever and ever.*

Daniel 12:3 NCV

🖎 Our world needs Christian leaders who "will
shine like stars forever and ever." Our world needs
leaders who willingly honor God with their words
and their deeds—with the emphasis on deeds.

If you seek to be a godly leader, then you must
begin by being a worthy example to your family,
to your friends, to your church, and to your
community. After all, your words of instruction
will never ring true unless you yourself are willing
to follow them.

Are you the kind of leader whom you would
want to follow? If so, congratulations. But if the
answer to that question is no, then it's time to
improve your leadership skills, beginning with the
words that you speak and the example that you
set. And the greatest of these, not surprisingly, is
example.

🖎 *Greatness lies not in being strong, but in the right
use of strength.*

Henry Ward Beecher

🖎 *Leadership is found in becoming the servant of all.*

Richard Foster

DISCOVERING GOD'S PURPOSE . . . AND DOING IT

If we live in the Spirit, let us also walk in the Spirit.
Galatians 5:25 NKJV

ॐ God has plans for your life, but He won't force His plans upon you. Your Creator has given you the ability to make decisions on your own. With that freedom comes the responsibility of living with the consequences of your choices.

If you seek to live in accordance with God's plan for your life, you will study His Word, you will be attentive to His instructions, and you will be watchful for His signs. You will associate with fellow believers who, by their words and actions, will encourage your own spiritual growth. You will assiduously avoid those two terrible temptations: the temptation to sin _and_ the temptation squander time. And finally, you will listen carefully, even reverently, to the conscience that God has placed in your heart.

God has glorious plans for your day and your life. So as you go about your daily activities, keep your eyes and ears open . . . as well as your heart.

ॐ _You cannot stay where you are and go with God. For you to do the will of God, you must adjust your life to Him, His purposes, and His ways._

Henry Blackaby

PRACTICAL CHRISTIANITY

As you have therefore received Christ Jesus the Lord, so walk in Him, rooted and built up in Him and established in the faith, as you have been taught, abounding in it with thanksgiving.

Colossians 2:6, 7 NKJV

As Christians, we must do our best to ensure that our actions are accurate reflections of our beliefs. Our theology must be demonstrated, not only by our words but, more importantly, by our actions. In short, we should be practical believers, quick to act whenever we see an opportunity to serve God.

Are you the kind of practical Christian who is willing to dig in and do what needs to be done *when* it needs to be done? If so, congratulations: God acknowledges your service and blesses it. But if you find yourself more interested in the fine points of theology than in the needs of your neighbors, it's time to rearrange your priorities. God needs believers who are willing to roll up their sleeves and go to work for Him. Count yourself among that number. Theology is a good thing *unless* it interferes with God's work. And it's up to you to make certain that *your* theology doesn't.

Had Jesus been the Word become word, He would have spun theories about life, but since he was the Word become flesh, he put shoes on all his theories and made them walk.

E. Stanley Jones

WORKING WITH HEART AND SOUL

He did it with all his heart. So he prospered.
2 Chronicles 31:21 NKJV

℞ How does God intend for us to work? Does He intend for us to work diligently or does He, instead, reward mediocrity? The answer is obvious. God has created a world in which hard work is rewarded and sloppy work is not. Yet sometimes, we may seek ease over excellence, or we may be tempted to take shortcuts when God intends that we walk the straight and narrow path.

Today, heed God's Word by doing good work. Wherever you find yourself, whatever your job description, do your work, and do it with all your heart. When you do, you will most certainly win the recognition of your peers. But more importantly, God will bless your efforts and use you in ways that only He can understand. So do your work with focus and dedication. And leave the rest up to God.

℞ *God never does anything for a man that the man can do for himself. The Lord is too busy for that. So look after your own business and let the Good Lord look after His.*

Sam Jones

THE POWER OF POSITIVE FRIENDSHIPS

Light shines on those who do right;
joy belongs to those who are honest.
Rejoice in the Lord, you who do right.
Praise his holy name.

Psalm 97:11, 12 NCV

⊳ If you'd like to build a positive life, find positive friends. If you'd like to live a godly life, seek the fellowship of godly friends. If you'd like to live passionately, prayerfully, and purposefully, spend time with people who are already living passionate, prayerful, purposeful lives. Soon, you'll soon discover that you will inevitably become more and more like the people who surround you day in and day out.

In choosing your friends, you set your course for the future. So choose carefully . . . very carefully.

⊳ *For better or worse, you will eventually become more and more like the people you associate with. So why not associate with people who make you better, not worse?*

Marie T. Freeman

⊳ *Nothing can be more dangerous than keeping wicked companions. They communicate the infection of their vices to all who associate with them.*

Jean Baptiste de la Salle

GOD IN HIS PROPER PLACE

You shall have no other gods before Me.

— _Exodus 20:3_ NKJV

℘ Who rules your heart? Is it God, or is it something else? Do you give God your firstfruits or your last? Have you given Christ your heart, your soul, your talents, your time, and your testimony? Or are you giving Him little more than a few hours each Sunday morning?

In the book of Exodus, God warns that we should place no gods before Him. Yet all too often, we place our Lord in second, third, or fourth place as we worship the gods of pride, greed, power, or personal gratification. When we unwittingly place possessions or relationships above our love for the Creator, we must seek His forgiveness and repent from our disobedience.

Does God rule your heart? Make certain that the honest answer to this question is a resounding yes. In the life of every righteous believer, God comes first. And that's precisely the place that He deserves in your heart.

℘ _As we find that it is not easy to persevere in this being "alone with God," we begin to realize that it is because we are not "wholly for God." God has a right to demand that He should have us completely for Himself._

Andrew Murray

WITH CHRISTLIKE HUMILITY

Let this mind be in you which was also in Christ Jesus,
who . . . made Himself of no reputation,
taking the form of a bondservant,
and coming in the likeness of men.

Philippians 2:5, 7 NKJV

℥ Dietrich Bonhoeffer observed, "It is very easy to overestimate the importance of our own achievements in comparison with what we owe others." How true. Even those of us who consider ourselves "self-made" men and women are deeply indebted to more people than we can count. Our first and greatest indebtedness is to God and His only begotten Son. But we are also indebted to ancestors, parents, teachers, friends, spouses, family members, coworkers, fellow believers…and the list goes on.

With so many people who rightfully deserve to share the credit for our successes, how can we gloat? The answer, of course, is that we should not.

Whenever you do good work, you are entitled to take pride in your accomplishments. But not too much pride. Instead of puffing out your chest and saying, "Look at me!", give credit where credit is due, starting with God. And rest assured: There is no such thing as a self-made man. All of us are made by God…and He deserves the glory, not us.

℥ *It was pride that changed angels into devils; it is humility that makes men as angels.*

St. Augustine of Hippo

THANKING GOD FOR HIS GIFTS

Thanks be to God for His indescribable gift!

2 Corinthians 9:15 NKJV

How do we thank God for the gifts He has given us? By using those gifts for the glory of His kingdom.

God has given you talents and opportunities that are uniquely yours. Are you willing to use your gifts in the way that God intends? And are you willing to summon the discipline that is required develop your talents and to hone your skills? That's precisely what God wants you to do, and that's precisely what *you* should desire *for yourself*.

As you seek to expand your talents, you will undoubtedly encounter stumbling blocks along the way, such as the fear of rejection or of failure. When you do, don't stumble! Just continue to refine your skills, and offer your services to God. And when the time is right, He will use you—but it's up to *you* to be thoroughly prepared when He does.

What we are is God's gift to us. What we become is our gift to God.

Anonymous

In gratitude for God's gift of life to us we should share that gift with others. The art of giving encompasses many areas. It is an outgoing, overflowing way of life.

Wilferd Peterson

Wed

PATIENCE AND TRUST

*Trust in Him at all times, you people; pour out
your heart before Him; God is a refuge for us.*

Psalm 62:8 NKJV

As individuals, as families, as businesses, and
as a nation, we are impatient for the changes
that we so earnestly desire. We want solutions
to our problems, and we want them right now!
But sometimes, life's greatest challenges defy easy
solutions, so we must be patient.

Psalm 37:7 commands us to "Rest in the Lord,
and wait patiently for Him" (NKJV). But for most
of us, waiting quietly for God is difficult. Why?
Because we are imperfect beings who seek solutions
to our problems today, if not sooner. We seek to
manage our lives according to our own timetables,
not God's. To do so is a mistake. Instead of
impatiently tapping our fingers, we should fold our
fingers and pray. When we do, our Heavenly Father
will reward us in His own miraculous way *and* in
His own perfect time.

*Let me encourage you to continue to wait with faith.
God may not perform a miracle, but He is trustworthy
to touch you and make you whole where there used to
be a hole.*

Lisa Whelchel

THE CHEERFUL GIVER

So let each one give as he purposes in his heart,
not grudgingly or of necessity;
for God loves a cheerful giver.

2 Corinthians 9:7 NKJV

☙ Are you a cheerful giver? If you intend to obey God's commandments, you must be. When you give, God looks not only at the quality of your gift, but also at the condition of your heart. If you give generously, joyfully, and without complaint, you obey God's Word. But, if you make your gifts grudgingly, or if the motivation for your gift is selfish, you disobey your Creator, *even* if you have tithed in accordance with Biblical principles.

Today, take God's commandments to heart and make this pledge: Be a cheerful, generous, courageous giver. The world needs your help, and you need the spiritual rewards that will be yours when you give faithfully, prayerfully, and cheerfully.

☙ *A cheerful giver does not count the cost of what he gives. His heart is set on pleasing and cheering him to whom the gift is given.*

Juliana of Norwich

☙ *A happy spirit takes the grind out of giving. The grease of gusto frees the gears of generosity.*

Charles Swindoll

THE WISDOM OF MODERATION

*But take heed to yourselves, lest your hearts
be weighed down with carousing, drunkenness,
and cares of this life.*

Luke 21:34 NKJV

🔊 Moderation and wisdom are traveling companions. If we are wise, we must learn to temper our appetites, our desires, and our impulses. When we do, we are blessed, in part, because God has created a world in which temperance is rewarded and intemperance is inevitably punished.

Would you like to improve your life? Then harness your appetites and restrain your impulses. Moderation is difficult, of course; it is *especially* difficult in a prosperous society such as ours. But the rewards of moderation are numerous and long-lasting. Claim those rewards today.

No one can force you to moderate your appetites. The decision to live temperately (and wisely) is yours and yours alone. And so are the consequences.

🔊 *To many, total abstinence is easier than perfect moderation.*

St. Augustine of Hippo

🔊 *Every moment of resistance to temptation is a victory.*

Frederick William Faber

LIVING IN THE SPIRIT OF TRUTH

But when the Spirit of truth comes,
he will lead you into all truth.

John 16:13 NCV

℘ God is vitally concerned with truth. His Word teaches the truth; His Spirit reveals the truth; His Son leads us to the truth. When we open our hearts to God, and when we allow His Son to rule over our thoughts and our lives, God reveals Himself, and we come to understand the truth about ourselves *and* the Truth about God's gift of grace.

The familiar words of John 8:32 remind us that "you shall know the truth, and the truth shall make you free" (NKJV). May we, as believers, seek God's truth and live by it, this day and forever.

℘ *Those who walk in truth walk in liberty.*

Beth Moore

℘ *The instrument of our sanctification is the Word of God. The Spirit of God brings to our minds the precepts and doctrines of truth, and applies them with power. The truth is our sanctifier. If we do not hear or read it, we will not grow in sanctification.*

C. H. Spurgeon

℘ *Truth will triumph. The Father of truth will win, and the followers of truth will be saved.*

Max Lucado

THE WISDOM OF THANKSGIVING

It is good to give thanks to the Lord,
and to sing praises to Your name, O Most High.

Psalm 92:1 NKJV

ॐ God's Word makes it clear: A wise heart is a thankful heart. Period. We are to worship God, in part, by the genuine gratitude we feel in our hearts for the marvelous blessings that our Creator has bestowed upon us. Yet even the most saintly among us must endure periods of bitterness, fear, doubt, and regret. Why? Because we are imperfect human beings who are incapable of perfect gratitude. Still, even on life's darker days, we must seek to cleanse our hearts of negative emotions and fill them, instead, with praise, with love, with hope, and with thanksgiving. To do otherwise is to be unfair to ourselves, to our loved ones, and to our God.

ॐ *Thanksgiving or complaining—these words express two contrastive attitudes of the souls of God's children in regard to His dealings with them. The soul that gives thanks can find comfort in everything; the soul that complains can find comfort in nothing.*

Hannah Whitall Smith

ॐ *We ought to give thanks for all fortune: if it is good, because it is good, if bad, because it works in us patience, humility, and the contempt of this world along with the hope of our eternal country.*

C. S. Lewis

LEARNING LIFE'S LESSONS . . .
THE EASY WAY

Whoever is stubborn after being corrected many times will suddenly be hurt beyond cure.

Proverbs 29:1 NCV

❧ When it comes to learning life's lessons, we can either do things the easy way or the hard way. The easy way can be summed up as follows: When God teaches us a lesson, we learn it . . . the first time! Unfortunately, too many of us learn much more slowly than that.

When we resist God's instruction, He continues to teach, whether we like it or not. Our challenge, then, is to discern God's lessons from the experiences of everyday life. Hopefully, we learn those lessons sooner rather than later because the sooner we do, the sooner He can move on to the next lesson and the next, and the next . . . .

❧ *What God asks of us is both simpler and more profound than adherence to a system of beliefs or following a set of rules. He asks us to walk with him through the blood and guts of our real experience in an honest pilgrimage where we let him show us what real strength, and real love, are all about.*

Paula Rinehart

THE POSITIVE PATH

But the path of the just is like the shining sun, that
shines ever brighter unto the perfect day. The way of
the wicked is like darkness; they do not know
what makes them stumble.

Proverbs 4:18, 19 NKJV

℘ When Jesus addressed His disciples, He warned
that each one must, "take up his cross and follow
me." The disciples must have known exactly what
the Master meant. In Jesus' day, prisoners were
forced to carry their own crosses to the location
where they would be put to death. Thus, Christ's
message was clear: In order to follow Him, Christ's
disciples must deny themselves and, instead, trust
Him completely. Nothing has changed since then.

If we are to be dutiful disciples of the One from
Galilee, we must trust Him and we must follow
Him. Jesus never comes "next." He is always first.
He shows us the path of life.

Do you seek to be a worthy disciple of Jesus?
Then pick up His cross today and follow in His
footsteps. When you do, you can walk with
confidence: He will never lead you astray.

℘ *Be such a person, and live such a life, that if every*
person were such as you, and every life a life like yours,
this earth would be God's Paradise.

Phillips Brooks

LIVING ABOVE THE DAILY WHINE

Do all things without complaining and disputing,
that you may become blameless and harmless,
children of God without fault in the midst of
a crooked and perverse generation,
among whom you shine as lights in the world.

Philippians 2:14, 15 NKJV

৯ Because we are imperfect human beings, we often lose sight of our blessings. Ironically, most of us have more blessings than we can count, but we may still find reasons to complain about the minor frustrations of everyday life. To do so, of course, is not only wrong; it is also the pinnacle of shortsightedness and a serious roadblock on the path to spiritual abundance.

Are you tempted to complain about the inevitable minor frustrations of everyday living? Don't do it! Today and every day, make it a practice to count your blessings, not your hardships. It's the truly decent way to live.

৯ _After one hour in heaven, we shall be ashamed that we ever grumbled._

Vance Havner

৯ _The last of the human freedoms is to choose one's attitude in any given set of circumstances._

Viktor Frankl

COMMENDING OURSELVES TO OTHERS

Therefore, since we have this ministry,
as we have received mercy, we do not lose heart.
But we have renounced the hidden things of shame,
not walking in craftiness nor handling the word
of God deceitfully, but by manifestation of
the truth commending ourselves to every
man's conscience in the sight of God.

2 Corinthians 4:1, 2 NKJV

God has given us a guidebook for righteous living called the Holy Bible. It contains thorough instructions which, if followed, lead to fulfillment, righteousness and salvation. But, if we choose to ignore God's commandments, the results are as predictable as they are unfortunate.

A righteous life has many components: faith, honesty, love, kindness, humility, gratitude, and worship, to name but a few. If we seek to follow the steps of our Savior, Jesus Christ, we must seek to live according to His commandments. In short, we must, to the best of our abilities, live according to the principles contained in God's Holy Word.

So today and every day of your life, study God's Word and live by it. Make your life a shining example for those who have not yet found Christ. Embrace righteousness; honor Your Heavenly Father by obeying Him.

Our Shepherd leads us in paths of righteousness—not for our name's sake but for His.

Elisabeth Elliot

RETURNING GOD'S LOVE . . .
BY SHARING IT

Beloved, if God so loved us,
we also ought to love one another.

1 John 4:11 NKJV

ℒ God loves you. How will you respond to His love? The Bible clearly defines what your response should be: "You shall love the Lord your God with all your heart, with all your soul, and with all your strength" (Deuteronomy 6:5 NKJV). But you must not stop there. You must also love your neighbor as yourself. Jesus teaches that "On these two commandments hang all the Law and the Prophets" (Matthew 22: 40).

Today, as you meet the demands of everyday living, will you pause long enough to return God's love? And then will you share it? Prayerfully, you will. When you embrace God's love, you are forever changed. When you embrace God's love, you feel differently about yourself, your family, your friends, and your world. When you embrace God's love, you have enough love to keep and enough love to share: enough love for a day, enough love for a lifetime, enough love for all eternity.

ℒ _Love is an attribute of God. To love others is evidence of a genuine faith._

Kay Arthur

BEYOND SELF-DECEPTION

*If we say that we have no sin, we deceive ourselves,
and the truth is not in us. If we confess our sins,
He is faithful and just to forgive us our sins
and to cleanse us from all unrighteousness.*

1 John 1:8, 9 NKJV

❧ If we deny our sins, we allow those sins to flourish. And if we allow sinful behaviors to become habits, we invite hardships into our own lives and into the lives of our loved ones. When we yield to the distractions and temptations of this troubled world, we suffer. But God has other intentions, and His plans for our lives do not include sin *or* denial.

When we allow ourselves to encounter God's presence, He will lead us away from temptation, away from confusion, and away from the self-deception. God is the champion of truth and the enemy of denial. May we see ourselves through His eyes and conduct ourselves accordingly.

❧ *Sin is largely a matter of mistaken priorities. Any sin in us that is cherished, hidden, and not confessed will cut the nerve center of our faith.*

Catherine Marshall

❧ *God has a plan and the devil has a plan, and you will have to decide which plan you are going to fit into.*

Billy Graham

LIVING WITH THE UNEXPECTED

Do not boast about tomorrow,
for you do not know what a day may bring forth.

Proverbs 27:1 NKJV

᪥ The old saying is both familiar and true: "Man proposes and God disposes." Proverbs 27:1 remind us that our world unfolds according to *God's* plans not *our* wishes. Thus, boasting about future events should to be avoided by believers who acknowledge God's sovereignty over all things.

Are you planning for a better tomorrow for yourself and your family? If so, you are to be congratulated: God rewards forethought in the same way that He often punishes impulsiveness. But, as you make your plans, do so with humility, with gratitude, and with trust in your heavenly Father. His hand directs the future; to think otherwise is both arrogant *and* naïve.

᪥ *That we may not complain of what is, let us see God's hand in all events; and, that we may not be afraid of what shall be, let us see all events in God's hand.*

Matthew Henry

᪥ *No matter how heavy the burden, daily strength is given, so I expect we need not give ourselves any concern as to what the outcome will be. We must simply go forward.*

Annie Armstrong

WHAT CAN I LEARN TODAY?

*It takes knowledge to fill a home with rare
and beautiful treasures.*

Proverbs 24:4 NCV

🐦 If we are to grow as Christians, we need both knowledge and wisdom. Knowledge is found in textbooks. Wisdom, on the other hand, is found in God's Holy Word and in the carefully-chosen words of loving parents, responsible family members, dedicated teachers, and trusted friends.

Knowledge is an important building block in a well-lived life, and it pays rich dividends both personally and professionally. But, wisdom is even more important because it refashions not only the mind, but also the heart.

🐦 *Today is yesterday's pupil.*

Thomas Fuller

🐦 *A big difference exists between a head full of knowledge and the words of God literally abiding in us.*

Beth Moore

🐦 *A little knowledge turns one away from God; a great deal of knowledge brings one back to him.*

Monica

PATIENCE WITH OTHERS
AND ONE'S SELF

God has chosen you and made you his holy people.
He loves you. So always do these things: Show mercy
to others, be kind, humble, gentle, and patient.
Colossians 3:12 NCV

№ Being patient with other people can be difficult.
But sometimes, we find it even more difficult to be
patient _with ourselves_. We have high expectations
and lofty goals. We want to accomplish things now,
not later. And, of course, we want our lives to unfold according to our own timetables, not God's.

Throughout the Bible, we are instructed that
patience is the companion of wisdom. Proverbs
16:32 teaches us that "Patience is better than
strength" (NCV). And, in 1 Peter 5:6, we are told to
"humble yourselves under the mighty hand of God,
that He may exalt you in due time" (NKJV).

God's message, then, is clear: We must be
patient with all people, beginning with that
particular person who stares back at us each time
we gaze into the mirror.

№ _The times we find ourselves having to wait on others_
may be the perfect opportunities to train ourselves to
wait on the Lord.

Joni Eareckson Tada

Wed

BEYOND OUR FEARS

But He said to them, "Why are you fearful,
O you of little faith?" Then He arose and rebuked
the winds and the sea, and there was a great calm.

Matthew 8:26 NKJV

℘ A frightening storm rose quickly on the Sea of Galilee, and the disciples were afraid. Because of their limited faith, they feared for their lives. When they turned to Jesus, He calmed the waters and He rebuked His disciples for their lack of faith in Him.

On occasion, we, like the disciples, are frightened by the inevitable storms of life. Why are we afraid? Because we, like the disciples, possess imperfect faith.

When we genuinely accept God's promises as absolute truth, when we trust Him with life here on earth *and* life eternal, we have little to fear. Faith in God is the antidote to worry. Faith in God is the foundation of courage and the source of power. Today, let us trust God more completely and, by doing so, move *beyond* our fears to a place of abundance, assurance, and peace.

℘ *Fear lurks in the shadows of every area of life. The future may look very threatening. Jesus says, "Stop being afraid. Trust me!"*

Charles Swindoll

INCLUDING GOD IN
THE PLANNING PROCESS

There is no wisdom, understanding,
or advice that can succeed against the Lord.

Proverbs 21:30 NCV

🔊 Does God have a plan for your life? Of course He does! Every day of your life, He is trying to lead you along a path of His choosing . . . but He won't force you to follow. God has given you free will, the opportunity to make decisions for yourself. The choices are yours: Either you will choose to obey His Word and seek His will, or you will choose to follow a different path.

Today, as you carve out a few quiet moments to commune with your Heavenly Father, ask Him to renew your sense of purpose. God's plans for you may be far bigger than you imagine, but He may be waiting for you to make the next move—so today, make that move prayerfully, faithfully, and expectantly. And after you've made _your_ move, trust God to make His.

🔊 _God wants to use us as He used His own Son._

Oswald Chambers

🔊 _The one supreme business of life is to find God's plan for your life and live it._

E. Stanley Jones

WISDOM IS AS WISDOM DOES

A foolish person enjoys doing wrong,
but a person with understanding
enjoys doing what is wise.

Proverbs 10:23 NCV

🐚 Do you seek to become wise? If so, you must behave wisely. Wisdom is as wisdom does.

High-sounding platitudes are as common as table salt. Aphorisms are everywhere. Parables proliferate. No matter. Wisdom is denominated not by words, but by deeds.

Do you wish to walk among the wise? If so, you must walk wisely. There is simply no other way.

🐚 *Wisdom is not wisdom when it is derived from books alone.*

Horace

🐚 *The best evidence of our having the truth is our walking in the truth.*

Matthew Henry

🐚 *Wisdom is the foundation, and justice is the work without which a foundation cannot stand.*

Ambrose

A New Life

You have been born again, and this new life did not come from something that dies, but from something that cannot die. You were born again through God's living message that continues forever.

2 Peter 1:23 NCV

❧ God's Word is clear: When we genuinely invite Him to reign over our hearts, and when we accept His transforming love, we are forever changed. When we welcome Christ into our hearts, an old life ends and a new way of living—along with a completely new way of viewing the world—begins.

Each morning offers a fresh opportunity to invite Christ, yet once again, to rule over our hearts and our days. Each morning presents yet another opportunity to take up His cross and follow in His footsteps. Today, let us rejoice in the new life that is ours through Christ, and let us follow Him, step by step, on the path that He first walked.

❧ *It is the secret of true discipleship to bear the cross, to acknowledge the death sentence that has been passed on self, and to deny any right that self has to rule over us.*

Andrew Murray

❧ *You were born with tremendous potential. When you were born again through faith in Jesus Christ, God added spiritual gifts to your natural talents.*

Warren Wiersbe

DREAMS NOT WORTH CHASING

Those who work their land will have plenty of food,
but the ones who chase empty dreams
instead will end up poor.

Proverbs 28:19 NCV

🔊 Some of our most important dreams are the ones we abandon. Some of our most important goals are the ones we don't attain. Sometimes, our most important journeys are the ones that we take to the winding conclusion of what seem to be to be a dead end streets. Thankfully, with God there are no dead ends; there are only opportunities to learn, to yield, to trust, to serve, and to grow.

The next time you experience one of life's inevitable disappointments, don't despair and don't be afraid to try "Plan B". Consider every setback an opportunity to choose a different, more appropriate path. Have faith that God may indeed be leading you in an entirely different direction, a direction of His choosing. And as you take your next step, remember that what looks like a dead end to you may, in fact, be the fast lane according to God.

🔊 *The maturity of a Christian experience cannot be reached in a moment, but is the result of the work of God's Holy Spirit, who, by His energizing and transforming power, causes us to grow up into Christ in all things.*

Hannah Whitall Smith

A LIFETIME OF SPIRITUAL GROWTH

You are God's children whom he loves,
so try to be like him. Live a life of love just as Christ
loved us and gave himself for us as a sweet-smelling
offering and sacrifice to God.

Ephesians 5:1 NCV

℘ The journey toward spiritual maturity lasts a lifetime: As Christians, we can and should continue to grow in the love and the knowledge of our Savior as long as we live. Norman Vincent Peale had simple advice for believers of all ages: "Ask the God who made you to keep remaking you." That advice, of course, is perfectly sound, but too often ignored.

When we cease to grow, either emotionally or spiritually, we do ourselves and our families a profound disservice. But, if we study God's Word, if we obey His commandments, and if we live in the center of His will, we will not be "stagnant" believers; we will, instead, be growing Christians . . . and that's exactly what God wants for our lives.

In those quiet moments when we open our hearts to God, the Creator who made us keeps remaking us. He gives us direction, perspective, wisdom, and courage. And, the appropriate moment to accept His spiritual gifts is always this one.

℘ *Growing in any area of the Christian life takes time,*
and the key is daily sitting at the feet of Jesus.

Cynthia Heald

BEYOND ANXIETY

Anxiety in the heart of man causes depression,
but a good word makes it glad.

Proverbs 12:25 NKJV

ஃ God calls us to live above and beyond anxiety. God calls us to live by faith, not by fear. He instructs us to trust Him completely, this day and forever. But sometimes, trusting God is difficult, especially when we become caught up in the incessant demands of an anxious world.

When you feel anxious—and you will—return your thoughts to God's love. Then, take your concerns to Him in prayer, and to the best of your ability, leave them there. Whatever "it" is, God is big enough to handle it. Let Him. Now.

ஃ *He treats us as sons, and all he asks in return is that we shall treat Him as a Father whom we can trust without anxiety. We must take the son's place of dependence and trust, and we must let Him keep the father's place of care and responsibility.*

Hannah Whitall Smith

ஃ *The thing that preserves a man from panic is his relationship to God.*

Oswald Chambers

THE BEGINNING OF KNOWLEDGE

The fear of the Lord is the beginning of knowledge,
but fools despise wisdom and instruction.

Proverbs 1:7 NKJV

⌘ God's hand shapes the universe, and it shapes our lives. God maintains absolute sovereignty over His creation, and His power is beyond comprehension. As believers, we must cultivate a sincere respect for God's awesome power. God has dominion over all things, and until we acknowledge His sovereignty, we lack the humility we need to live righteously, and we lack the humility we need to become wise.

The fear of the Lord is, indeed, the beginning of knowledge. So today, as you face the realities of everyday life, remember this: Until you acquire a healthy, respectful fear of God's power, your education is incomplete, and so is your faith.

⌘ *Remember that this fear of the Lord is His treasure, a choice jewel, given only to favorites, and to those who are greatly beloved.*

John Bunyan

⌘ *God does not give His counsel to the curious or the careless; He reveals His will to the concerned and to the consecrated.*

Warren Wiersbe

YOUR PARTNERSHIP WITH GOD

*God is working in you to help you want to do
and be able to do what pleases him.*

Philippians 2:13 NCV

🐚 Do you seek a life of purpose, abundance, and fulfillment? If so, then you must form a partnership with God.

You are God's work-in-progress. God wants to mold your heart and guide your path, but because He created you as a creature of free will, He will not force you to become His. That choice is yours alone, and it is a choice that should be reflected in every decision you make *and* every step you take.

Today, as you encounter the challenges of everyday life, strengthen your partnership with God through prayer, through obedience, through praise, through thanksgiving, and through service. God is the *ultimate* partner, and He wants to be *your* partner in every aspect of your life. Please don't turn Him down.

🐚 *No matter what we are going through, no matter how long the waiting for answers, of one thing we may be sure. God is faithful. He keeps His promises. What he starts, He finishes . . . including His perfect work in us.*

Gloria Gaither

GUARDING OUR HEARTS AND MINDS

*And the peace of God, which surpasses all
understanding, will guard your hearts and minds
through Christ Jesus. Finally, brethren, whatever
things are true, whatever things are noble, whatever
things are just, whatever things are pure, whatever
things are lovely, whatever things are of good
report, if there is any virtue and if there is anything
praiseworthy—meditate on these things.*

Philippians 4:7, 8 NKJV

ॐ You are near and dear to God. He loves you
more than you can imagine, and He wants the very
best for you. And one more thing: God wants you
to guard your heart.

Every day, you are faced with choices . . . lots of
them. You can do the right thing, or not. You can
walk with the Lord, or not. You can be kind, and
generous, and obedient. Or not.

Today, the world will offer you countless
opportunities to let down your guard and, by doing
so, let the devil do his worst. Be watchful and
obedient. Guard your heart by giving it to your
Heavenly Father; it is safe with Him.

ॐ *Prayer guards hearts and minds and causes God to
bring peace out of chaos.*

Beth Moore

FAITH WITHOUT WORKS

What does it profit, my brethren, if someone says he has faith but does not have works? Can faith save him? If a brother or sister is naked and destitute of daily food, and one of you says to them, "Depart in peace, be warmed and filled," but you do not give them the things which are needed for the body, what does it profit? Thus also faith by itself, if it does not have works, is dead.

James 2:14–17 NKJV

℘ The central message of James' letter is the need for believers to act upon their beliefs. James' instruction is clear: "faith without works is dead." We are saved by our faith in Christ, but salvation does not signal the end of our earthly responsibilities; it marks the true beginning of our work for the Lord.

If your faith in God is strong, you will find yourself drawn toward God's work. You will serve Him, not just with words or prayers, but also with deeds. Because of your faith, you will feel compelled to do God's work—to do it gladly, faithfully, joyfully, and consistently.

Today, redouble your efforts to do God's bidding here on earth. Never have the needs—or the opportunities—been greater.

℘ *We are saved by faith alone, but faith is never alone.*

John Calvin

WHAT GOD REQUIRES

*He has shown you, O man, what is good; And what
does the LORD require of you but to do justly,
to love mercy, and to walk humbly with your God?*

Micah 6:8 NKJV

❧ What does God require of us? That we worship Him only, that we welcome His Son into our hearts, and that we walk humbly with our Creator.

When Jesus was tempted by Satan, the Master's response was unambiguous. Jesus chose to worship the Lord and serve Him only. We, as followers of Christ, must follow in His footsteps.

When we place God in a position of secondary importance, we do ourselves great harm and we put ourselves at great risk. But when we place God squarely in the center of our lives—when we walk humbly and obediently with Him—we are blessed and we are protected.

❧ *Let us remember therefore this lesson: That to worship our God sincerely we must evermore begin by hearkening to His voice, and by giving ear to what He commands us.*

John Calvin

❧ *In the great orchestra we call life, you have an instrument and a song, and you owe it to God to play them both sublimely.*

Max Lucado

THE LOVE OF MONEY . . .

For the love of money is a root of all kinds of evil,
for which some have strayed from the faith
in their greediness, and pierced themselves
through with many sorrows.

1 Timothy 6:10 NKJV

✍ Our society is in love with money and the things that money can buy. God is not. God cares about people, not possessions, and so must we. We must, to the best of our abilities, love our neighbors as ourselves, and we must, to the best of our abilities, resist the mighty temptation to place possessions ahead of people.

Money, in and of itself, is not evil; *worshipping* money is. So today, as you prioritize matters of importance for you and yours, remember that God is almighty, but the dollar is not. If we worship God, we are blessed. But if we worship "the almighty dollar", we are inevitably punished because of our misplaced priorities—and our punishment inevitably comes sooner rather than later.

✍ *Theirs is an endless road, a hopeless maze, who seek for goods before they seek for God.*

Bernard of Clairvaux

✍ *Why is love of gold more potent than love of souls?*

Lottie Moon

COURAGE IS CONTAGIOUS

I will lift up my eyes to the hills—
From whence comes my help? My help comes
from the Lord, Who made heaven and earth.

Psalms 121:1, 2 NKJV

℘ The more we trust God, the more courageously we live. And the more we trust God, the more we can encourage others.

Courage is contagious, and courage inspired by a steadfast trust in a loving Heavenly Father is *highly* contagious. Today, as you interact with friends, family members, or coworkers, share your courage, your hopes, your dreams, and your enthusiasm. Your positive outlook will be almost as big a blessing *to them* as it is *to you*.

℘ *Just as courage is faith in good, so discouragement is faith in evil, and, while courage opens the door to good, discouragement opens it to evil.*

Hannah Whitall Smith

℘ *We are either the masters or the victims of our attitudes. It is a matter of personal choice.*

John Maxwell

℘ *Attitude is more important than the past, than education, than money, than circumstances, than what people do or say. It is more important than appearance, giftedness, or skill.*

Charles Swindoll

GODLY THOUGHTS, GODLY ACTIONS

Commit your works to the Lord,
and your thoughts will be established.

Proverbs 16:3 NKJV

ℬ Our thoughts have the power to lift us up or drag us down; they have the power to energize us or deplete us, to inspire us to greater accomplishments or to make those accomplishments impossible.

God intends that you experience joy and abundance, but He will not impose His joy upon you; you must accept it for yourself. It's up to you to celebrate the life that God has given you by focusing your mind upon "whatever is of good repute" (Philippians 4:8) Today, spend more time thinking about God's blessings, and less time fretting about the minor inconveniences of life. Then, take time to thank the Giver of all things good for gifts that are glorious, miraculous, and eternal.

ℬ *The greatest discovery of my generation is that people can alter their lives by altering their attitudes of mind.*

William James

ℬ *Whenever a negative thought concerning your personal power comes to mind, deliberately voice a positive thought to cancel it out.*

Norman Vincent Peale

THE POWER OF WILLING HANDS

A lazy person will end up poor,
but a hard worker will become rich.

Proverbs 10:4 NCV

God's Word teaches us the value of hard work. In his second letter to the Thessalonians, Paul warns, "…if anyone will not work, neither shall he eat" (3: 10 NKJV). And the Book of Proverbs proclaims, "A person who doesn't work hard is just like someone who destroys things" (18:9 NCV). In short, God has created a world in which diligence is rewarded but sloth is not. So, whatever it is that you choose to do, do it with enthusiasm and dedication.

Hard work is not simply a proven way to get ahead, it's also part of God's plan for you. God did not create you for a life of mediocrity; He created you for far greater things. Reaching for greater things usually requires work and lots of it, which is perfectly fine with God. After all, He knows that you're up to the task, and He has big plans for you *if* you possess a loving heart and willing hands.

If, in your working hours, you make the work your end, you will presently find yourself all unawares inside the only circle in your profession that really matters. You will be one of the sound craftsmen, and other sound craftsmen will know it.

C. S. Lewis

FAITHFULNESS AND FOCUS

*You will seek the Lord your God,
and you will find Him if you seek Him
with all your heart and with all your soul.*

Deuteronomy 4:29 NKJV

✍ God deserves your best. Is He getting it? Do you make an appointment with your Heavenly Father each day? Do carve out moments when He receives your undivided attention? Or is your devotion to Him fleeting, distracted, and sporadic?

When you acquire the habit of focusing your heart and mind squarely upon God's intentions for your life, He will guide your steps and bless your endeavors. But if you allow distractions to take priority over your relationship with God, they will—and you will pay a price for your mistaken priorities.

Today, focus upon God's Word and upon His will for your life. When you do, you'll be amazed at how quickly *everything else* comes into focus, too.

✍ *Christian discipleship is a process of paying more and more attention to God's righteousness and less and less attention to our own; finding the meaning of our lives not by probing our moods and motives and morals, but by believing in God's will and purposes.*

Eugene Peterson

UNDERSTANDING THE GREATNESS OF CHRIST'S LOVE

And I pray that you and all God's holy people will have the power to understand the greatness of Christ's love—how wide and how long and how high and how deep that love is. Christ's love is greater than anyone can ever know, but I pray that you will be able to know that love. Then you can be filled with the fullness of God.

Ephesians 3:18, 19 NCV

ℤ Christ's love for you is personal. He loves you so much that He gave His life in order that you might spend all eternity with Him. Christ loves you individually and intimately; His is a love unbounded by time or circumstance. Are you willing to experience an intimate relationship with Him? Your Savior is waiting patiently; don't make Him wait a single minute longer. Embrace His love today. Fill yourself with the fullness of God.

ℤ *Christ is like a river that is continually flowing. There are always fresh supplies of water coming from the fountain-head, so that a man may live by it and be supplied with water all his life. They who live upon Christ may have fresh supplies from him for all eternity.*

Jonathan Edwards

LABORING FOR THE MASTER

Then He said to His disciples,
"The harvest truly is plentiful,
but the laborers are few."

Matthew 9:37 NKJV

How will you honor God today? Will you honor Him with the best you have to offer? Will you tithe the firstfruits of your harvest? Will you praise God not only with your words but also with your deeds? If you do, you will be blessed by a loving and righteous Father.

Each day provides a fresh opportunity to honor God with your prayers, with your praise, with your testimony, and with your service. Does the level of your stewardship honor the One who has given you everything? If so, rest assured: God will bless you because of your obedience. And if your stewardship has been somehow deficient, the best day to change is this one.

If God has called you, do not spend time looking over your shoulder to see who is following you.

Corrie ten Boom

You can sing your heart out but never give back to God, and you'll miss the fullness of worship.

Dave Ramsey

FAITH ON FIRE

*I tell you the truth, whoever believes in me will do
the same things that I do. Those who believe
will do even greater things than these,
because I am going to the Father.*

John 14:12 NCV

🕮 John Wesley advised, "Catch on fire with
enthusiasm and people will come for miles to watch
you burn." His words still ring true. When we fan
the flames of enthusiasm for Christ, our faith serves
as a beacon to others.

Our world desperately needs faithful believers
who share the Good News of Jesus with joyful exu-
berance. Be such a believer. The world desperately
needs your enthusiasm, and just as importantly, *you*
need the experience of sharing it.

🕮 *There seems to be a chilling fear of holy enthusiasm
among the people of God. We try to tell how happy we
are—but we remain so well-controlled that there are
very few waves of glory experienced in our midst.*

A. W. Tozer

🕮 *Your enthusiasm will be infectious, stimulating, and
attractive to others. They will love you for it. They will
go for you and with you.*

Norman Vincent Peale

STEWARDSHIP OF GOD'S GIFTS

As each one has received a gift,
minister it to one another, as good stewards of
the manifold grace of God.

1 Peter 4:10 NKJV

The gifts that you possess are gifts from the Giver of all things good. Do you have a spiritual gift? Share it. Do you have a testimony about the things that Christ has done for you? Don't leave your story untold. Do you posses financial resources? Share them. Do you particular talents? Hone your skills and use them for God's glory.

When you hoard the treasures that God has given you, you live in rebellion against His commandments. But, when you obey God by sharing His gifts freely and without fanfare, you invite Him to bless you more and more. Today, be a faithful steward of your talents and treasures. And then prepare yourself for *even greater* blessings that are sure to come.

You are the only person on earth who can use your ability.

Zig Ziglar

It is the definition of joy to be able to offer back to God the essence of what he's placed in you, be that creativity or a love of ideas or a compassionate heart or the gift of hospitality.

Paula Rinehart

FAIRNESS AND HONEST DEALINGS

The Lord hates dishonest scales,
but he is pleased with honest weights.

Proverbs 11:1 NCV

It has been said on many occasions and in many ways that honesty is the best policy. For believers, it is far more important to note that honesty is God's policy. And if we are to be servants worthy of our savior, Jesus Christ, we must be honest and forthright in our communications with others.

Sometimes, honesty is difficult; sometimes, honesty is painful; but honesty is *always* God's commandment. In the Book of Exodus, God did not command, "Thou shalt not bear false witness *when* it is convenient." And He didn't say, "Thou shalt not bear false witness *most* of the time." God said, "Thou shalt not bear false witness against thy neighbor." Period.

Sometime soon, perhaps even today, you will be tempted to bend the truth or perhaps even to break it. Resist that temptation. Truth is God's way…and it must also be yours. Period.

The single most important element in any human relationship is honesty—with oneself, with God, and with others.

Catherine Marshall

DEFEATING THOSE
EVERYDAY FRUSTRATIONS

Foolish people are always fighting,
but avoiding quarrels will bring you honor.

Proverbs 20:3 NCV

❧ Anger is a natural human emotion that is sometimes necessary and appropriate. Even Jesus became angry when confronted with the moneychangers in the temple (Matthew 21). Righteous indignation is an appropriate response to evil, but God does not intend that anger should rule our lives. Far from it. God intends that we turn away from anger whenever possible and forgive our neighbors just as we seek forgiveness for ourselves.

Life is full of frustrations, both big and small. On occasion, you, like Jesus, will confront evil, and when you do, you may respond as He did: vigorously and without reservation. But more often, your frustrations will be of the more mundane variety: a traffic jam, a spilled cup of coffee, an inconsiderate comment, a broken promise. When you are tempted to lose your temper over the minor inconveniences of life, don't. Turn away from anger, hatred, bitterness, and regret. Turn instead to God. When you do, you'll be following His commandments *and* giving yourself a priceless gift, the gift of peace.

❧ *Why lose your temper if, by doing so, you offend God, annoy other people, give yourself a bad time . . . and, in the end, have to find it again?*

Josemaria Escriva

Enough Is Enough

*Let your conduct be without covetousness; be content
with such things as you have. For He Himself
has said, "I will never leave you nor forsake you."*

Hebrews 13:5 NKJV

⚞ Ours is a world that glorifies material possessions.
Christians, of course, should not. As believers who
have been touched and transformed by the grace
of a risen Savior, we must never allow the things
of this earth to distance us from our sense of God's
presence and the direction of God's hand. If we
are to enjoy the peace and abundance that God
has promised us, we must reign in our desire for
more and more; we must acknowledge that when
it comes to earthly possessions, enough is always
enough.

⚞ *Contentment is possible when we stop striving for
more.*

Charles Swindoll

⚞ *When you accept rather than fight your circumstances, even though you don't understand them, you
open your heart's gate to God's love, peace, joy, and
contentment.*

Amy Carmichael

FINDING PURPOSE THROUGH SERVICE

> *But he who is greatest among you*
> *shall be your servant.*
>
> Matthew 23:11 NKJV

❦ If you genuinely seek to discover God's unfolding purpose for your life, you must ask yourself this question: "How does God want me to serve others?"

Whatever your path, whatever your calling, you may be certain of this: Service to others is an integral part of God's plan for your life. Christ was the ultimate servant, the Savior who gave His life for mankind. As His followers, we, too, must become humble servants.

Every single day of your life, including this one, God will give you opportunities to serve Him by serving His children. Welcome those opportunities with open arms. They are God's gift to you, His way of allowing you to achieve greatness in His kingdom.

❦ *Service is the pathway to real significance.*

Rick Warren

❦ *In the very place where God has put us, whatever its limitations, whatever kind of work it may be, we may indeed serve the Lord Christ.*

Elisabeth Elliot

BEYOND BLAME

When they continued to ask Jesus their question,
he raised up and said, "Anyone here who has
never sinned can throw the first stone at her."

John 8:7 NCV

❧ To blame others for our own problems is the
height of futility. Yet blaming others is so easy to
do and improving ourselves is so much harder.
So instead of solving problems ourselves, we are
tempted to do otherwise; we are tempted to fret
over the perceived unfairness of life while doing
precious little else.

Are you looking for an ironclad formula for problem-solving that will leave you happier, healthier,
wealthier, and wiser? Here it is: don't play the blame
game—because to play it is to lose it.

❧ *The main thing is this: we should never blame*
anyone or anything for our defeats. No matter how evil
their intentions may be, they are altogether unable to
harm us until we begin to blame them and use them as
excuses for our own unbelief.

A. W. Tozer

❧ *You'll never win the blame game, so why even bother*
to play?

Marie T. Freeman

A PERFECT TIMETABLE

He has made everything beautiful in its time.
Also He has put eternity in their hearts.

Ecclesiastes 3:11 NKJV

❧ Upon this we can trust: God's sense of timing is without error. God's timing may not coincide with *our* timing—which, by the way, is perfectly fine with God because *He* knows precisely what He's doing, even if *we* do not.

Perhaps you are impatient for God to reveal His plans for your life. If so, it is time to reread the third chapter of Ecclesiastes. Solomon's words will remind you that there is a time for every purpose under God's heaven—and that includes *your* purpose.

❧ God is concerned about your life through eternity. Allow Him to take all the time He needs to shape you for His purposes. Larger assignments will require longer periods of preparation.

Henry Blackaby

❧ The only thing that can hinder us is our own failure to work in harmony with the plans of the Creator, and if this lack of harmony can be removed, then God can work.

Hannah Whitall Smith

In Search of a Quiet Conscience

My child, if sinners try to lead you into sin,
do not follow them.

Proverbs 1:10 NCV

❧ American humorist Josh Billings observed, "Reason often makes mistakes, but conscience never does." How true. Even when we deceive our neighbors, and even when we attempt to deceive ourselves, God has given each of us a conscience, a small, quiet voice that tells us right from wrong. We must listen to that inner voice . . . or else we must accept the consequences that inevitably befall those who choose to rebel against God.

❧ _One of the ways God has revealed Himself to us is in the conscience. Conscience is God's lamp within the human breast._

Billy Graham

❧ _To go against one's conscience is neither safe nor right. Here I stand. I cannot do otherwise._

Martin Luther

❧ _A quiet conscience sleeps in thunder._

Thomas Fuller

❧ _He that loses his conscience has nothing left that is worth keeping._

Izaak Walton

Wed

LOOKING AHEAD

Do not remember the former things,
nor consider the things of old.
Behold, I will do a new thing.

Isaiah 43:18, 19 NKJV

❧ Just as a garden is dormant in winter, so too, does the human soul endure seasons when growth is restrained. But just as springtime returns to the flowers to the garden, so too, does hope return to the human soul . . . in time.

Sometimes, the demands of daily life can drain us of our strength and rob us of the joy that is rightfully ours in Christ. But on our darkest days, God stands ready to renew our spirits and restore our strength.

God can make all things new, including you. Your job is to let Him.

❧ *God is not running an antique shop! He is making all things new!*

Vance Havner

❧ *No matter how badly we have failed, we can always get up and begin again. Our God is the God of new beginnings.*

Warren Wiersbe

LOVING GOD AND OTHERS

Jesus said to him, "You shall love the Lord your God with all your heart, with all your soul, and with all your mind. This is the first and great commandment. And the second is like it: 'You shall love your neighbor as yourself.' On these two commandments hang all the Law and the Prophets."

Matthew 22:37–40 NKJV

❦ Christ's words leave no room for interpretation: He instructs us to love the Lord with all our hearts and to love our neighbors as we love ourselves. But sometimes, despite our best intentions, we fall short. When we become embittered with ourselves, with our neighbors, or most especially with God, we disobey the One who gave His life for us. And we bring inevitable, needless suffering into our lives.

If we are to please God, we must cleanse ourselves of the negative feelings that separate us from others *and* from Him. In 1 Corinthians 13, we are told that love is the foundation upon which all our relationships are to be built—our relationships with others *and* our relationship with our Creator. May we fill our hearts with love; may we never yield to bitterness. And may we praise the Son of God who, in His infinite wisdom, made love His greatest commandment.

❦ *The nearer we draw to God in our love for him, the more we are united together by love for our neighbor.*

Dorotheus of Gaza

WORSHIPPING THE RISEN CHRIST

He is not here, but is risen!

Luke 24:6 NKJV

God has a wonderful plan for your life, and an important part of that plan includes worship. We should never deceive ourselves: Every life is based upon some form of worship. The question is not *whether* we worship, but *what* we worship.

Some of us choose to worship God. The result is a plentiful harvest of joy, peace, and abundance. Others distance themselves from God by foolishly worshiping earthly possessions and personal gratification. To do so is a mistake of profound proportions.

Have you accepted the grace of God's only begotten Son? Then worship Him. Worship Him today and every day. Worship Him with sincerity and thanksgiving. Write His name on your heart and rest assured that He, too, has written *your* name on His.

Abide in Jesus, the sinless one—which means, give up all of self and its life, and dwell in God's will and rest in His strength. This is what brings the power that does not commit sin.

Andrew Murray

FINISHING THE WORK

It is better to finish something than to start it.
It is better to be patient than to be proud.

Ecclesiastes 7:8 NCV

❧ As you continue to seek God's purpose for your life, you will undoubtedly experience your fair share of disappointments, detours, false starts, and failures. When you do, don't become discouraged: God's not finished with you yet.

The old saying is as true today as it was when it was first spoken: "Life is a marathon, not a sprint." That's why wise travelers select a traveling companion who never tires and never falters. That partner, of course, is your Heavenly Father.

Are you tired? Ask God for strength. Are you discouraged? Believe in His promises. Are you defeated? Pray as if everything depended upon God, and work as if everything depended upon you. And finally, have faith that you play important role in God's great plan for mankind—because you do.

❧ *Let us not cease to do the utmost, that we may incessantly go forward in the way of the Lord; and let us not despair.*

John Calvin

❧ *The value of good work depends on perseverance. You live a good life in vain if you do not continue it until you die.*

Gregory

For God So Loved the World

For God so loved the world that He gave
His only begotten Son, that whoever believes in Him
should not perish but have everlasting life.

John 3:16 NKJV

✸ For believers, death is not an ending; it is a beginning. For believers, the grave is not a final resting-place, it is a place of transition. For believers, death is not a dark journey into nothingness; it is a homecoming.

God sent His Son as a sacrifice for our sins. Through Jesus, we are redeemed. By welcoming Christ into our hearts, we have received the precious, unfathomable gift of eternal life. Let us praise God for His Son. The One from Galilee has saved us from our sins so that we might live courageously, die triumphantly, and live again—eternally.

✸ *O God, Thou hast made us for Thyself, and our hearts are restless until they find their rest in Thee.*

St. Augustine of Hippo

✸ *Considering how I prepare for my children when I know they are coming home, I love to think of the preparations God is making for my homecoming one day. He knows the colors I love, the scenery I enjoy, the things that make me happy, all the personal details.*

Anne Graham Lotz

GOD IS LOVE

And we have known and believed the love that God has for us. God is love, and he who abides in love abides in God, and God in him.

1 John 4:16 NKJV

❧ St. Augustine observed, "God loves each of us as if there were only one of us." Do you believe those words? Do you seek to have an intimate, one-on-one relationship with your Heavenly Father, or are you satisfied to keep Him at a "safe" distance?

Sometimes, in the crush of our daily duties, God may seem far away, but He is not. God is everywhere we have ever been and everywhere we will ever go. He is with us night and day; He knows our thoughts and our prayers. And, when we earnestly seek Him, we will find Him because He is here, waiting patiently for us to reach out to Him. Let us reach out to Him today and always. And let us praise Him for the glorious gifts that have transformed us today and forever. Amen.

❧ *The love of God is one of the great realities of the universe, a pillar upon which the hope of the world rests. But it is a personal, intimate thing too. God does not love populations. He loves people. He loves not masses, but men.*

A. W. Tozer

REFLECTIONS